FOREWORD

CW01500529

by Martin A. Armstrong

Kerry Lutz has put to̶g̶e̶t̶h̶e̶r̶ a̶ c̶o̶m̶p̶i̶l̶a̶t̶i̶o̶n̶ of interviews he has conducted with me over the years. He was surprised at how accurate my predictions have been and had me on his podcast to talk about it. We forged a fast friendship, and in subsequent years, I enjoyed many appearances on Kerry's podcast. The forecasts that I made in these interviews with Kerry are not my personal opinion. They were the result of early artificial intelligence technology that I designed back in the 1980s. I had an unusual background in computer science in hardware and software and applied my knowledge to finance and global markets.

My first exposure to international finance was in 1965 when my father took the family to Europe for the summer. We traveled everywhere, from Sweden to Italy. When crossing the border back then, it was necessary to change your currency. That taught me about foreign exchange, and it also taught me that currency was a mental language of value. You had to constantly convert whatever currency you were dealing with back to your home currency to judge value.

Because I was the first independent analyst to forecast currencies, and I was accurate, governments, multinational corporations, and international investors became interested in my predictions and soon demanded this service worldwide. The AI's a track record of accurately predicting not just financial markets, but it has been able to forecast political elections and even wars.

I happened to have a client who was an executive VP at Franklin National Bank, which was the first banking failure after the collapse of the Bretton Woods monetary system of fixed currencies in 1971. He asked me for help figuring out if the problem may have been tangled up in currency. Indeed, the bank failed because of a major shift in the

1

Italian lira. After that, when a problem would emerge regarding foreign exchange, it seemed like someone would always say, "Get that guy that did Franklin National Bank."

Back then, I was providing daily reports on initially gold, and then it expanded into currencies. These reports had to go out by telex, and the communication costs were huge. I thought I would open an office in Geneva, yet I knew there was anti-Americanism. I went to lunch with one of the heads of one of the top three Swiss banks. I had a list of European names and asked him his opinion on which name I should use. He asked me to name one European analyst, and I could not. He laughed and told me that was because there weren't any. He remarked that I did not know why all the institutions were using my services. I replied no. He then said that I did not care if the dollar went up or down. I said it was just a trade. He then explained that because the politicians had used the rise in their currencies against the dollar as proof that they did a good job, no analyst could say a country's currency would decline because that would be considered a political statement.

It was back in the early 1980s that a major bank in Lebanon found a ledger where someone had written down the value of the Lebanese pound every day into the mid-19th century. They asked if I would create a model on their currency. I put the data into the computer and out came a forecast that their country would fall apart in eight days. I thought there was something wrong with the data. I told the client, and they calmly asked what currency would be best to convert to. I said the Swiss franc.

I did not understand the fundamentals at the time. I thought their response was strange. Sure enough, precisely eight days later, on June 6th, 1982, the civil war began. I came to realize that they did not come to me for the forecast. They already saw the money moving. They came to me for the timing. I came to realize that someone always knows about a war in advance, and assets start to move. My computer was

THE WORLD ACCORDING TO MARTIN ARMSTRONG

CONVERSATIONS WITH THE MASTER FORECASTER

Kerry Lutz

Foreword by Martin Armstrong

THE WORLD ACCORDING TO MARTIN ARMSTRONG:
CONVERSATIONS WITH THE MASTER FORECASTER

Editing and cover by George Verongos

Paperback ISBN: 979-8-998545497-0-9

Hardback ISBN: 979-8-998545497-1-6

Digital ISBN: 979-8-998545497-2-3

7890
PUBLISHING

Content

monitoring capital flows to ascertain the shifts internationally in capital investments. It was able to forecast the collapse of Russia in 1998.

I learned to view the world through my clients' eyes, colored by their currency. I came to understand that the global economy is complex, but its movement was entirely predicated upon the interaction of everyone, for we are all connected. The US was virtually bankrupt in 1896 when JP Morgan had to bail out the US Treasury with a $100 million gold loan. By the end of World War II, the US had 76% of the official gold reserves. If it had not been for Europe blowing their brains out twice, in theory, Americans would still be mostly farmers.

INTRODUCTION: THE CONVERSATION BEGINS

I first heard about Martin Armstrong through the writings of the late James Sinclair. Sinclair described Martin as a political prisoner, wrongly held and grossly mistreated by the government for more than a decade. Despite these extraordinary threats and challenges to his safety, Martin managed to produce a newsletter from within prison, which gained a wide audience in the outside world. While the production values of his work were understandably limited, consisting of hand-drawn charts and typewritten text, the insights he offered were nothing short of extraordinary. Concepts like the Economic Confidence Model (ECM) and the Global Flow of Funds were entirely unique at the time and were not discussed anywhere else.

Martin was a renowned economist and monetary expert long before his imprisonment. He had mastered the complexities of the floating exchange rate currency markets well before they became widely understood. His expertise brought him into consultation with politicians, central bankers, and global power players. Highly successful, his rise was meteoric—until, in an instant, his company was driven into bankruptcy, and he was imprisoned for contempt of court. Ultimately, he spent more than 11 years in prison. Martin says, "They wanted my programs, but I refused and never turned them over, despite long stretches of solitary confinement and their ceaseless attempts to break me."

If you're skeptical of the existence of the "deep state" or the systemic corruption within institutions like the Department of Justice (Martin calls it the Department of Just Us), consider this: the Assistant U.S. Attorney overseeing the criminal division of New York's Southern District during Martin's ordeal was none other than James Comey. A coincidence? Perhaps.

I first spoke to Martin several months after his release. I was surprised by the person I encountered. I expected bitterness, anger and resentment, but instead, I found a gentle, thoughtful man who seemed at peace, remarkably free of animosity towards those who had persecuted him. At the time, I had no idea that this conversation would spark a 14-year friendship and an ongoing dialogue that continues to this day.

Martin's forecasts have been remarkably accurate, as the transcripts in this book will show. He is perhaps best known for his prescient calls on major market crashes, including the 1987 Black Monday crash, the 1989 Nikkei collapse, and the Russian financial crisis of 1998. More recently, he accurately predicted the Swiss National Bank's 2015 decision to abandon the euro peg—a move that shocked global markets. Among his most audacious predictions was the Dow Jones Industrial Average's exponential rise over the past 14 years. While other *experts* have consistently predicted market crashes and a prolonged bear market, Martin had a different take. When our conversation started in late 2011, the Dow was hovering near 12,000 points, and Martin made the audacious forecast of Dow 35,000, Dow 45,000 (between 2022 and 2024), and even Dow 65,000 by 2032. As implausible as these forecasts were at the time, they came to pass. Remarkably, Dow 45,000 happened on December 4, 2024, right within Martin's time frame.

From our earliest discussions, Martin has been adamant that the U.S. dollar would maintain its dominance and reserve currency status well into the late 2020s and early 2030s. While many have speculated about the rise of alternative currencies or systems, Martin has consistently held that no viable competitor to the dollar currently exists. He does, however, foresee a potential shift by the early 2030s, with China emerging as the world reserve currency holder. At the same time, he has been unequivocally bearish about the prospects of the BRICS nations effectively supplanting the dollar, citing their lack of cohesion, trust, and scale required to sustain such a transition. And he has been equally dismissive of the Euro, believing in the inevitability of its collapse.

In addition to his Dow calls, Martin has made numerous predictions about gold, housing, and inflation—many of which have come to pass. His Economic Confidence Model, which identifies cyclical patterns in economic activity, has become a cornerstone of his forecasting and has proven remarkably reliable over the decades.

This book captures an over one decade-long conversation with one of the most enigmatic and brilliant forecasters of our time. Through these interviews and insights, I hope to share Martin's unparalleled perspective on economics, history, and the cycles that shape our world. Doubt his predictions at your own risk; Martin Armstrong's record speaks for itself.

WHO IS MARTIN ARMSTRONG?

Martin A. Armstrong, the founder of Socrates and Armstrong Economics, is an internationally recognized economist and former hedge fund manager with over 40 years of experience monitoring and forecasting market behavior. Originating from his passion for researching monetary history and a determination to harness the power of computers and artificial intelligence, Mr. Armstrong has built an innovative collection of proprietary models that help identify market patterns in an unbiased, data-driven approach. His models are available to the public under Socrates—the first software-as-a-service platform offering unique perspectives and tools intended to help individuals and organizations better research and interpret the global economic and political environment.

The models Armstrong has built, including the Economic Confidence Model, which establishes the basic units of a business cycle as waves that build in 8.6-year intervals, have consistently proven that the global economy is not random. This has become one of the most important long-term forecasting models available today. Over the years, Martin has built additional independent models, such as Market Reversals, Forecast Arrays, and the Global Market Watch—each taking a slightly different view of pattern and cycle recognition. These models, while independent from each other, do have corollary benefits and are built from the ground up to consume mass amounts of information in order to learn and adapt continuously.

In the past, Martin Armstrong has been called upon by governments and major banking institutions to assist in the explanation of current events and their impact on the global economy. His forecasting has run in the face of traditional, narrow, fundamental views that fail to contemplate the business cycle and human behavior that drives it. Far too often, forecasting suffers from prejudice and preconceived notions. Analysts can manipulate data to paint just about any picture they want, whether consciously or subconsciously, rather than let the data paint its own picture. AE Global Solutions, Inc., Socrates, and Armstrong Economics were founded on the principles of observing history to understand the future.

Armstrong studied computer science in the 1960s when computers were the size of a room. He learned both electrical engineering and software development during his time at RCA Institute. By the time RCA sold their computer division to IBM, Armstrong had decided to leave the technology field and return to trading.

Martin soon realized that since he was trained in both hardware and software, he could design and create a program to help him hedge and trade. He got his inspiration for the software from a film in his 9th-grade history class about the Panic of 1869. "...*The Toast of New York* that had opened my eyes to the fact that there was not a linear progression to markets and economy but a cyclical rhythm. I knew that gold had been fixed in value at $35 an ounce, and in the film, there was a scene where Jim Fisk turns to his girlfriend and quotes gold at $162 an ounce. That introduced me to the idea that there were economic cycles."

Armstrong pursued his studies of economics, searching for answers behind the cycle of boom and busts that plagued society both in Princeton and in London. He began to do forecasting as a service to institutional cash market players in gold, including Swiss banks. As currency also began to float in 1971, Armstrong found the gyrations thought-provoking and began to notice the same oscillations that appeared in stocks in 1966, real estate into 1970, and gold as it rose to

$42 in 1968 and fell below the official price of $35 in 1970, were also manifesting in the rise and fall of currency prices. This realization led him to become one of the very first to begin forecasting currencies.

Martin Armstrong's models blend mathematics, history, and psychology to predict market behavior. The ECM and Socrates system are central to his work, offering a cyclical lens on economics and geopolitics. Despite skepticism, his theories remain influential in niche financial circles, illustrating the enduring appeal of cyclical explanations for complex phenomena.

Websites:

Socrates: www.Ask-Socrates.com

Public blog: ArmstrongEconomics.com

THE FRAGILE STATE OF THE GLOBAL FINANCIAL SYSTEM (DECEMBER 9, 2011)

Interview Summary:

Martin Armstrong dissects the unstable state of the global economic and financial system. The conversation addresses the flaws in the Eurozone, the unsustainable practices of global debt, and the ripple effects of corruption within regulatory and financial institutions. Armstrong provides insights into the inherent instability of the Euro, the dangers of over-leveraging client assets, and the inevitability of systemic collapse unless fundamental changes are implemented.

Martin Armstrong: Thank you for inviting me.

Kerry Lutz: Martin, how are we doing?

Martin Armstrong: Fine, how have you been?

Kerry Lutz: Great, great. Your last appearance went over big—we got tens of thousands of downloads. I'm glad you found time to come back with us. I know you just wrapped up a February conference that was standing-room only. The word's getting out, huh?

Martin Armstrong: Yes, it's been surprising. Normally, we limit our conferences to 100–125 people, but this time, we had to accommodate 300 attendees and still turned away another 365. It's more a reflection of the times than of me, honestly.

Kerry Lutz: What's your diagnosis and prognosis for the Euro? The media seems full of disinformation—what's really going on?

Martin Armstrong: My political sources in Europe tell me there's a small minority—maybe 5–7% of those in government—who truly understand the situation and want to enact meaningful change. However, Germany is at a critical crossroads. They'll eventually face a choice: let the Euro collapse or inflate their way out. My sources confirm Germany will opt for inflation.

Kerry Lutz: What choice do they have? Merkel wouldn't want to be remembered as the leader who caused a global banking panic. She'll kick the can down the road until it's someone else's problem.

Martin Armstrong: That's exactly it. The coalition government in Germany knows they'd lose an election today, so they're holding on. Meanwhile, land and firewood in Germany are selling out because people are preparing for what they see as the end of the world. German public opinion is overwhelmingly against Merkel's policies; they'd prefer to let the Euro collapse.

Kerry Lutz: It seems Germany's history of hyperinflation during the Weimar era shapes their resistance to inflationary policies.

Martin Armstrong: Absolutely. Germany's economic philosophy centers on austerity, but the reality is they'll have to inflate. This goes against their cultural and historical instincts, but it's the only path forward. It's akin to America choosing austerity—it's just not in the national DNA.

Kerry Lutz: The current system seems broken. Isn't it time for something new?

Martin Armstrong: The Euro was doomed from the start because it lacks a unified debt structure. When forming the currency, policymakers dismissed my advice. They initially wanted one interest rate for all member countries, which would have caused immediate collapse. Instead, they allowed each country to issue its own bonds, creating a system where traders could exploit weaker economies like

Greece or Spain. Essentially, they shifted currency volatility to bond markets, but it's the same problem.

Kerry Lutz: So, despite the shared currency, it operates like multiple currencies because each country issues its own debt.

Martin Armstrong: Exactly. Traders can short the bonds of specific countries like Greece or Italy, which mimics shorting their currencies. The Eurozone failed to create a true single currency. Imagine if U.S. states issued debt that served as bank reserves—chaos would ensue.

Kerry Lutz: Cheap money in countries like Spain fueled unsustainable booms. Now what? How do they clean this up?

Martin Armstrong: They'll keep kicking the can down the road. Ultimately, the world needs a functional monetary system, but policymakers lack the vision to build one. Governments keep borrowing, and today's bonds—unlike savings bonds of the past—can be used as collateral, making debt indistinguishable from money.

Kerry Lutz: The debt is unsustainable. What happens when the bubble bursts?

Martin Armstrong: We're nearing that tipping point. Germany recently failed to sell all its bonds at auction—a critical red flag. When governments can no longer sell debt, the game is over. At that point, Germany and others will have no choice but to print money, effectively monetizing debt.

Kerry Lutz: So they become the buyer of last resort.

Martin Armstrong: Precisely. It's like writing yourself a trillion-dollar check and moving it from one pocket to another. That's what central banks will do—issue debt and buy it themselves.

Kerry Lutz: On another note, how does the collapse of MF Global fit into this larger picture?

Martin Armstrong: MF Global highlights systemic corruption. For decades, firms have used client assets as collateral without proper disclosure. This practice became routine by the mid-1980s. The MF Global collapse is particularly troubling because the CME, which acts as a clearinghouse, failed to back client trades. Clients who weren't even trading—just holding T-bills—have had their money frozen.

Kerry Lutz: It's shocking how pervasive this is.

Martin Armstrong: It is. What's worse, MF Global lobbied to block regulations that would have protected client funds. This was no accident—there's deep corruption within financial institutions, regulators, and the courts. If the public understood the extent of this, it could trigger widespread panic.

Kerry Lutz: So, it's all about maintaining appearances?

Martin Armstrong: Exactly. The system relies on confidence, but it's built on shaky foundations. If people lose trust, the entire structure collapses.

Kerry Lutz: Thanks for breaking this down, Martin. Where can listeners find you?

Martin Armstrong: Visit ArmstrongEconomics.com, or email me at martinarmstrongeconomics@hotmail.com.

Kerry Lutz: Thanks again, Martin. We'll check in with you after the New Year. Have a great holiday season.

Key Takeaways:

1. **Eurozone Instability:** The Euro was flawed from its inception due to its lack of unified debt management. Each country issues its own debt, creating disparities that allow traders to exploit weaker economies like Greece and Spain.

Germany, historically wary of inflation, faces a critical choice: allow the Euro to collapse or inflate its way out. Signs of public panic in Germany, such as land and firewood hoarding, reflect deep concerns about economic stability.

2. **Global Debt Dynamics:** The global financial system is over-leveraged, with government bonds functioning as bank reserves and international collateral. This has made debt indistinguishable from money.

   The U.S. national debt, largely driven by interest payments, would be significantly lower if money had been printed rather than borrowed. The current system creates perpetual debt cycles.

3. **Systemic Corruption:** Practices such as rehypothecation of client funds have been common since the 1980s, leading to disasters like the MF Global collapse. Regulatory agencies like the SEC have failed to act, often swayed by political lobbying.

   The financial system's reliance on undisclosed leveraging creates massive off-balance-sheet risks, exacerbating instability.

4. **Impending Collapse:** Signs of strain include Germany's recent failure to sell all of its bonds in an auction, a critical red flag. The inability to sell debt marks the point of no return for economic systems.

   The global financial system is on a trajectory toward hyperinflation, as governments likely opt to inflate rather than deflate, given the unpopularity of austerity measures.

Final Thought:

The global financial system is teetering on the edge of collapse, with its foundation riddled with flaws, corruption, and unsustainable debt practices. While governments continue to kick the can down the road, hyperinflation looms as the probable outcome. Meaningful reform is unlikely without systemic failure, leaving individuals and institutions to brace for the fallout of this precarious economic order.

Dominoes of Debt: The Global Financial Unraveling (June 14, 2012)

Interview Summary:

This conversation delves into the instability of the global financial system, focusing on cascading debt crises in Europe and beyond. Martin Armstrong discusses how sovereign debt defaults create capital flight to perceived safe havens, temporarily strengthening the dollar while destabilizing other currencies. With a historical perspective on economic collapses, Armstrong connects past patterns to current trends, including government overreach, rising taxes, and electronic surveillance. He advises individuals to safeguard their wealth with tangible assets and anticipates a turning point by 2017 when the dollar may weaken and commodities could surge.

Kerry Lutz: Right now, the world is in complete flux. The dominoes are falling, but it's not clear in which direction. To help us make sense of it all, Martin Armstrong is here to discuss the latest developments, the ongoing collapses, and his highly anticipated upcoming book, which I've had the pleasure of previewing. It's compelling. Martin Armstrong, welcome back to *The Financial Survival Network*.

Martin Armstrong: Thank you, Kerry Lutz. It's always a pleasure to be here.

Kerry Lutz: You've been busy writing your book, and it seems like everything you're writing about is happening in real-time. Is that fair to say?

Martin Armstrong: Pretty much. The biggest confusion people have is expecting everything to happen at once. But it doesn't work that way. It's like a chain reaction with dominoes—one pushes the next, and so on. A couple of months ago, I said the "flight to quality" isn't over yet. During the Great Depression, as one country failed, capital moved to the next, eventually driving the dollar to extreme highs while Europe, South America, and China defaulted. It's a sequential process, and the U.S. is always the last stop.

Kerry Lutz: So you're saying big money moves differently than the average individual?

Martin Armstrong: Exactly. Large institutions can't just pull $10 billion out of a bank in cash. They need to park it somewhere, usually in government debt. That's why U.S. Treasury yields are at record lows—it's the safest option amid global turmoil. For example, France just elected a socialist president promising a 75% tax on the wealthy, driving capital flight to Switzerland. Meanwhile, governments globally are becoming increasingly aggressive, raising taxes and fines and ramping up enforcement in desperate attempts to plug their deficits.

Kerry Lutz: Like jaywalking tickets in Manhattan?

Martin Armstrong: Exactly. In New Jersey, they've ramped up seatbelt law enforcement after decades of neglect. It's less about safety and more about generating revenue. Now, with surveillance cameras issuing automated tickets, the government can collect fines without assigning points or going through court processes.

Kerry Lutz: Surveillance is everywhere now. In New York, for example, there's a camera on every corner near Penn Station. It's like we're living in an electronic police state.

Martin Armstrong: It's alarming. At a conference in Philadelphia, international attendees were shocked to learn they must provide fingerprints just to enter the U.S. The U.S. is building databases on everyone entering the country, something not even done to its own citizens. Add to that the crackdown on Americans opening foreign bank accounts—it's almost impossible now because foreign banks don't want to deal with U.S. regulations.

Kerry Lutz: So where does this leave things like gold and silver? Can they serve as protection against government overreach?

Martin Armstrong: For individuals, yes. But hedge funds and institutions are less likely to take physical positions in gold. During the 1934 gold confiscation, institutions handed over their holdings. I think gold will rally eventually, likely around 2017, when global confidence in the U.S. begins to waver. But until then, we're in a consolidation phase. Stocks and private-sector investments may be better hedges for institutional money as capital moves away from public debt.

Kerry Lutz: You've mentioned inflation is the ultimate outcome of this monetary policy. When will we see it manifest?

Martin Armstrong: Inflation will rise once asset deflation subsides. Right now, capital destruction from deleveraging is offsetting the Fed's monetary expansion. But once deleveraging ends and asset prices rise, inflation will take off—likely starting in 2014 and accelerating through 2017.

Kerry Lutz: Is there anywhere left in the world that's safe to live or invest?

Martin Armstrong: Some Southeast Asian countries and former communist states are better positioned—they don't have the same debt burdens. Debt is the root cause of this global turmoil. Governments are aggressively targeting their citizens for taxes, believing that collecting what they think is "owed" will solve the problem. But their spending outpaces revenue anyway.

Kerry Lutz: Do you think civil unrest is inevitable?

Martin Armstrong: Yes, as seen in Southern Europe. Governments' desperation will lead to unrest everywhere, including here in the U.S. They're already preparing—look at laws like the internet kill switch, which aims to prevent organized protests like those seen during the Arab Spring.

Kerry Lutz: Your upcoming book tackles these issues. Who is it written for?

Martin Armstrong: It's for the average person, not academics. My goal is to dispel myths, especially about events like the Great Depression. Most mainstream accounts ignore critical factors, like the sovereign debt crisis of 1931, which devastated Europe, South America, and China. I've relied on primary sources, including Herbert Hoover's memoirs, to present an accurate picture.

Kerry Lutz: That's fascinating. When will it be available?

Martin Armstrong: John Wiley plans to release it before the election, though the title hasn't been finalized. The book focuses on global economics, not just the U.S., and highlights how crises are often misrepresented by governments and media.

Kerry Lutz: Martin Armstrong, your insights are always invaluable. When the book is out, we'll have you back on to dive deeper. In the meantime, where can listeners read more of your work?

Martin Armstrong: They can visit ArmstrongEconomics.com.

Kerry Lutz: Thanks for joining us, Martin Armstrong. We'll talk again soon.

Martin Armstrong: Thank you, Kerry Lutz. Take care.

Gold Prices (2011 - 2024)

23

THE DEBT CRISIS AND POLITICAL PARALYSIS IN 2013 (DECEMBER 27, 2012)

Interview Summary:

Martin Armstrong shares insights on the global economic challenges heading into 2013. The conversation covers Southeast Asia's booming economy, Europe's failing policies, and the U.S.'s looming debt crisis. Armstrong warns of potential civil unrest if meaningful economic reform is ignored. He critiques misplaced tax policies that benefit bondholders at the expense of economic growth, highlights the pitfalls of unsustainable debt, and advocates for direct government funding as a solution to reduce debt burdens.

Kerry Lutz: Welcome back to *The Financial Survival Network*, Martin.

Martin Armstrong: Thank you for having me, Kerry.

Kerry Lutz: Always great to have you. We're heading for quite a difficult year in 2013, right?

Martin Armstrong: Yes, 2013 is shaping up to be pretty challenging. 2012 might feel calm by comparison.

Kerry Lutz: You've been traveling the world, observing all of this firsthand. What's your take on the global landscape?

Martin Armstrong: I recently finished a three-month tour through Hong Kong, Beijing, Southeast Asia, and Europe. Southeast Asia and China are still booming, and five of the top cities with the highest real economic growth are in China. Despite some misconceptions, there's real demand and development there, unlike in the U.S., which Southeast Asia is already largely writing off—they've shifted around 40% of their trade to China.

Kerry Lutz: And how does Europe compare?

Martin Armstrong: Europe's a different story—still struggling. Switzerland, for instance, is rolling back its historic banking secrecy laws, initially enacted to protect Germans from Hitler's anti-outside-account laws. And France? They're raising taxes on the wealthy to 75%, which is driving people out, and they've lowered the retirement age despite unfunded liabilities. Overall, the region's leadership lacks direction.

Kerry Lutz: It sounds like a mess everywhere. Then there's the U.S. and the looming "fiscal cliff."

Martin Armstrong: Yes, the U.S. is facing a major issue. Boehner nearly made a deal with Obama last year but backed off to keep his speakership. Now, Obama isn't interested, and the administration still believes raising taxes will help. But nearly 70% of the national debt is cumulative interest, most of it going to bondholders, including 40% overseas. Raising taxes isn't the solution—it's just feeding money to bankers.

Kerry Lutz: So, is the answer to repudiate the debt? What do you think?

Martin Armstrong: Not necessarily repudiation. We could either inflate our way out or default. But raising taxes is counterproductive, leading to less revenue as it shrinks the economy. The real challenge is that so much debt is held by pensions, so a default would collapse the entire pension system. We need a real solution instead of just taxing and sending interest overseas, which boosts economies like China.

Kerry Lutz: It's amazing. So is the idea of "taxing the rich to help the poor" just a myth?

Martin Armstrong: Yes, it's ineffective. Most of the money goes out of the country or back to bondholders. And the term "rich" keeps changing; today, it includes any household making over $250,000.

Kerry Lutz: And meanwhile, the average family on assistance in the U.S. ends up with benefits around $60,000, more than the average middle-class income.

Martin Armstrong: Yes, and this has long been a way to buy votes— vote for me, and I'll give you someone else's money. But we're running out of "other people's money."

Kerry Lutz: That's true. Margaret Thatcher warned us about that.

Martin Armstrong: In Europe, I noticed that entrepreneurship is thriving in the South, where people rely on it for survival, often operating off the books. In contrast, in Germany, the regulatory environment makes hiring nearly impossible, so entrepreneurship there is almost dead.

Kerry Lutz: We may see something similar here in the U.S. With so few job opportunities, people are starting businesses out of necessity.

Martin Armstrong: Yes, and the internet is enabling this. But it's also because governments globally are becoming more draconian. Many people are starting businesses online to avoid some of the bureaucracy.

Kerry Lutz: And you've proposed a solution that doesn't involve taxes. Can you elaborate?

Martin Armstrong: Yes, if we simply printed money instead of borrowing it, the national debt would be a third of its current size. It's cheaper and avoids interest payments. Canada used to do this. Today, we're effectively paying interest on printed money.

Kerry Lutz: So, instead of borrowing, we print to finance government spending?

Martin Armstrong: Exactly. Jefferson argued that there should be no national debt. He compromised with Hamilton, who insisted on one with conditions—it had to be paid off. If we'd stuck with that, we wouldn't be here.

Kerry Lutz: And things haven't improved since Jefferson's time.

Martin Armstrong: No, and history keeps repeating because human behavior doesn't change.

Kerry Lutz: Our system prioritizes short-term gains over long-term planning, unfortunately.

Martin Armstrong: Yes, and politicians care more about the next election than about real reforms. The structure of our system almost guarantees short-term thinking.

Kerry Lutz: Where do you see metals going in 2013?

Martin Armstrong: We're still in a consolidation phase until about August. Major turning points are coming in January, May, and June, but we won't see big moves in metals until late summer. Gold is a hedge against government instability, not inflation.

Kerry Lutz: So, consolidation until summer, then potentially more action?

Martin Armstrong: Yes, metals will likely strengthen as debt defaults become more visible, particularly in Europe. They're an alternative to government-backed currency.

Kerry Lutz: Retirement accounts and 401ks are often seen as targets. Do you think they're at risk?

Martin Armstrong: They are, especially given the current administration's view that individuals "don't deserve" such savings. Our system predicts the potential rise of a strong third-party movement by 2016 based on economic issues rather than ideological divides.

Kerry Lutz: I think both political parties are imploding right now. Without the other, neither party can exist for long, and the Republicans' November loss will likely lead to the collapse of both parties.

Martin Armstrong: I agree. The law passed last December, requiring foreign entities to report on U.S. citizens' financial activities or face confiscation, has had a massive impact. Americans are essentially being shut out of foreign banking.

Kerry Lutz: So the only entities able to do business overseas are big multinationals?

Martin Armstrong: Exactly. And now, as marijuana becomes legalized, we'll see big corporations dominate because it's easier for the government to manage.

Kerry Lutz: Well, Martin, thank you as always. Your conference is coming up in Philadelphia in March?

Martin Armstrong: Yes, March 13th.

Kerry Lutz: Great. We'll be there. Thanks for sharing your insights— always a pleasure.

Martin Armstrong: Thank you very much.

Key Takeaways:

1. **Global Economic Divide:** Southeast Asia and China are experiencing growth, while Europe and the U.S. struggle under failing policies and mounting debt.
2. **Taxation Myths:** High taxes and "tax the rich" policies are counterproductive and primarily benefit bondholders rather than the poor.
3. **Alternative Solutions:** Printing money directly instead of borrowing could reduce debt without causing inflation.
4. **Metals Outlook:** Gold and other metals will consolidate until late summer, then strengthen as debt crises escalate.
5. **Retirement Risks:** 401ks and retirement accounts remain vulnerable to government intervention.

Final Thought:

The year 2013 brings looming challenges, particularly in Europe and the U.S., where political paralysis and poor fiscal policies threaten economic stability. Tangible solutions like direct funding and reforming tax systems are crucial to long-term recovery.

Echoes of the Past: Europe's Financial Crisis and the Global Debt Dilemma (March 14, 2013)

Interview Summary:

In this early interview, Martin Armstrong explores Europe's financial instability, drawing parallels to the Panic of 1837 in the United States. He examines the structural weaknesses of the eurozone's single-currency model, the ripple effects of political inaction, and the historical lessons from decentralized U.S. banking. Armstrong highlights the global movement of capital toward the U.S. and the inevitability of government defaults, suggesting a "debt jubilee" as a potential solution.

Kerry Lutz: I'm Kerry Lutz, and with us now is Martin Armstrong. Martin, you've compared Europe's current crisis to the Panic of 1837 in the U.S. Can you explain why?

Martin Armstrong: Thanks for having me, Kerry. Yes, there's a strong parallel. Just like in 1837, when President Andrew Jackson dismantled the Second Bank of the United States and triggered financial instability, Europe's eurozone faces a structural crisis. The issue lies in launching the euro without consolidating debt. Leaders knew this was a problem but deferred it. Now, Southern Europe is suffocating under debt that's effectively doubled in cost due to the euro's rise.

Kerry Lutz: So, history repeating itself?

Martin Armstrong: Absolutely. After Jackson dismantled the central bank, U.S. state banks proliferated, issuing their own currencies, which destabilized the economy. Many states bailed out failing banks with bonds, leading to widespread defaults. Europe has a single currency but lacks fiscal unity, making it even more precarious.

Kerry Lutz: And now capital is fleeing Europe?

Martin Armstrong: Yes, instability in Europe and Japan has driven capital into the U.S., which is seen as a relatively safe haven. The German elections will play a key role in determining the euro's future, but the euro's structural flaws make it unsustainable without debt consolidation.

Kerry Lutz: Is a "debt jubilee" the only way out?

Martin Armstrong: It might be. Throughout history, governments eventually default on debt. Adam Smith observed this in *The Wealth of Nations*. Today, about 70% of U.S. national debt is accumulated interest. We're borrowing with no real intention of repaying the principal—it's unsustainable.

Kerry Lutz: So, borrowing is now just about rolling over debt endlessly?

Martin Armstrong: Exactly. Bonds no longer function as they once did. Inflation erodes the value of repayments, making long-term government debt a poor investment. Meanwhile, municipal defaults, like Detroit's, are increasingly likely as local governments overpromise without financial expertise.

Kerry Lutz: Should individuals leverage debt, then?

Martin Armstrong: Yes, long-term fixed-rate loans, like 30-year mortgages, are a hedge against inflation. Rising interest rates and a stronger dollar will only widen the gap between debt and asset values.

Kerry Lutz: And Europe?

Martin Armstrong: Without fiscal unity, Europe faces more debt crises. Southern Europe will likely see devaluations. Germany's austerity push clashes with France's resistance and Italy's focus on protecting citizens over bondholders. This division keeps capital fleeing to the U.S.

Kerry Lutz: Fascinating insights, Martin. Thanks for joining us.

Martin Armstrong: Thank you, Kerry. Always a pleasure.

Key Takeaways:

1. Europe's debt crisis mirrors the U.S. Panic of 1837, with structural instability due to decentralized fiscal policies.
2. The eurozone's failure to consolidate debt when launching the euro is a critical flaw, exacerbating economic disparities.
3. Capital is fleeing unstable regions like Europe and Japan, finding safety in U.S. equities and real estate.
4. A global "debt jubilee" may be necessary to reset the economic system and address unsustainable government borrowing.
5. Long-term fixed-rate loans are a hedge against inflation and rising interest rates.

Final Thought:

As Europe faces mounting debt and internal divisions, Armstrong's historical analysis underscores the urgent need for systemic reform to avoid repeating past financial crises.

BANK HOLIDAYS, FINANCIAL TYRANNY, AND THE CASE FOR TANGIBLE ASSETS (APRIL 11, 2013)

Interview Summary:

In this discussion, Kerry Lutz interviews economist Martin Armstrong about the increasing instability of the global financial system and the looming potential for widespread civil unrest. Armstrong explains how governments may resort to "bank holidays" and asset seizures to cover debts, drawing parallels to historical practices of forced loans. He highlights the growing importance of tangible assets like gold, silver, real estate, and stocks in navigating financial uncertainty and critiques alternative currencies like Bitcoin. The conversation provides a sobering look at the future of economic stability.

Kerry Lutz: Welcome to *The Financial Survival Network*. Are you ready for a bank holiday? Because if you don't decide to take a break from your bank, they just might decide to take a break from you. With events like Cyprus still fresh in mind, is it possible this could happen here in the U.S., or in other parts of Europe? To find out, there's only one person we can turn to, and that's Martin Armstrong. Martin, welcome back.

Martin Armstrong: Thanks for having me, Kerry.

Kerry Lutz: So, what's happening globally? Are we headed toward mass protests and bank runs, or will governments simply clamp down and refuse to let people withdraw their money?

Martin Armstrong: There are definitely signs pointing that way. What happened in Cyprus was a real warning shot, but actually, the first indication was MF Global. People assume that when they deposit money in a brokerage, it's secure and separate from the firm's debts, but that line got crossed. After the U.S. bailout, governments realized they couldn't just keep printing money for banks. Now, they're seriously looking at taking depositor funds directly—a practice historically known as "forced loans."

Kerry Lutz: So, just like in medieval times when citizens were compelled to buy government debt?

Martin Armstrong: Exactly. Back then, city-states like Venice and Florence mandated citizens to buy government debt. Today, with electronic banking, it's even easier—they can simply freeze withdrawals, convert a percentage to government bonds, and say, "Here's your bond." Cyprus was a test, really, to see how much they could get away with, but it's just escalating tensions instead of solving the root issues.

Kerry Lutz: And instead of reforming, governments are preparing for civil unrest, buying large quantities of ammunition and even tanks for domestic agencies.

Martin Armstrong: Yes, it's concerning. Governments seem focused on keeping power at all costs. We're seeing anti-democratic tendencies, especially in Europe. Countries are blocking referendums whenever they sense public opposition to policies. They'd rather enforce unpopular measures than listen to their citizens.

Kerry Lutz: And in the U.S., the financial system feels stacked against citizens, too. Just look at how attempts to hold banks accountable are consistently dismissed in courts. It feels like justice is completely one-sided.

Martin Armstrong: It is. In New York City, lawsuits against banks or agencies like the SEC are nearly always dismissed. When people sued the SEC for failing to act on Madoff, the court simply dismissed the case. There's a double standard at play, and this immunity extends to the banking system.

Kerry Lutz: Europe's banking system is particularly fragile because there's no consolidated national debt, and banks are pressured to buy bonds from every country.

Martin Armstrong: Right, which undermines stability. In the U.S., banks hold federal bonds as reserves, which are more secure. If banks here were forced to hold bonds from every state and states like California or New York defaulted, it would jeopardize the entire system.

Kerry Lutz: And we've seen what happens when collateral backing loans is suddenly downgraded, like in the repo market with mortgage-backed securities.

Martin Armstrong: Exactly. That's a 24-hour market, so if collateral suddenly loses value, everything unravels quickly. People should be cautious about storing wealth in assets the government can easily seize or control.

Kerry Lutz: Do you think people will simply accept these measures? Or is that why governments are stocking up on tanks and ammunition?

Martin Armstrong: Precisely. Governments see what's happening in Europe. Even the U.S. State Department issued an advisory suggesting Greece could see a revolution. But instead of addressing core issues, governments protect banks to ensure they'll continue selling government debt.

Kerry Lutz: And the idea of a gold standard keeps coming up, but you've mentioned before that it wouldn't solve the underlying debt issues.

Martin Armstrong: A gold standard sounds good, but it doesn't prevent reckless spending. The real issue is debt. Borrowing is just a delayed tax, and as debt grows, they'll keep coming back to raise taxes, which affects everyone. We need to cut off borrowing altogether.

Kerry Lutz: It's like a theme park ride where you pay to get on and then get charged again to get off. The whole system seems designed to trap people.

Martin Armstrong: Exactly. And if we'd simply printed money instead of borrowing, the national debt would be a third of what it is today. Seventy percent of our debt is interest—money that goes nowhere productive.

Kerry Lutz: So, in your view, where does this leave the average person? Should they be considering assets outside the banking system?

Martin Armstrong: Yes, absolutely. Tangible assets like gold, silver, real estate, and certain stocks offer security that can survive currency transitions. Even silver coins are better than relying on a financial system that might not hold.

Kerry Lutz: And this brings us to alternative currencies like Bitcoin. Is there a chance Bitcoin might become a serious alternative?

Martin Armstrong: Bitcoin has good intentions, but realistically, the government won't ignore it. In the late 1970s, tax straddles were popular until the IRS cracked down on them retroactively. Bitcoin could easily face similar treatment; governments won't allow any currency they can't control.

Kerry Lutz: So, your advice is to stick to tangible investments—gold, silver, real estate, and certain stocks—as these are the most secure in turbulent times.

Martin Armstrong: Exactly. These assets can carry value through economic shifts, which is essential when dealing with currency instability. Once people realize their currency is unreliable, they'll rush to convert it into hard assets—anything, even basic goods, to avoid holding depreciating currency.

Kerry Lutz: Fascinating insights, Martin. We're excited to hear more at the Liberty Mastermind Symposium this June. Thank you for joining us today.

Martin Armstrong: Thanks for having me, Kerry. Looking forward to it.

Key Takeaways:

1. **Banking Instability:** Governments are increasingly considering depositor asset seizures and financial restrictions, as seen in Cyprus.
2. **Tangible Assets for Security:** Gold, silver, real estate, and certain stocks are critical investments to protect against financial system failures.
3. **Debt Issues Persist:** A gold standard would not address the fundamental problems of runaway debt and reckless government spending.
4. **Bitcoin's Vulnerability:** While promising, Bitcoin faces potential government crackdowns, making tangible assets more reliable.

Final Thought:

Amid growing economic uncertainty, individuals must proactively secure their financial future through tangible investments. As history repeats itself with forced loans and asset seizures, preparation is the key to stability.

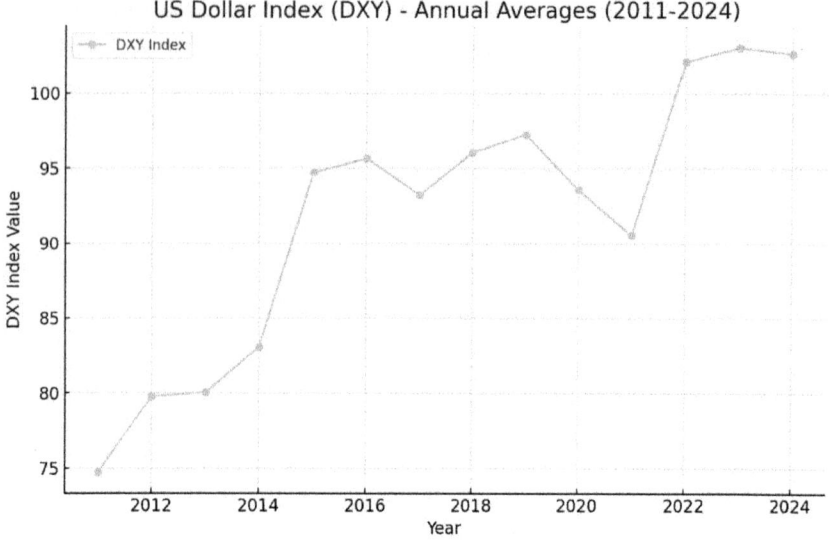

US Dollar Index (DXY) - Annual Averages (2011-2024)

THE GLOBAL FINANCIAL SQUEEZE: CURRENCY, DEBT, AND ECONOMIC VOLATILITY (MAY 21, 2013)

Interview Summary:

Martin Armstrong provides an in-depth analysis of escalating financial instability, focusing on currency volatility, government debt, and global economic shifts. Armstrong outlines how crises in Europe and the U.S. are interconnected and what these pressures mean for future financial stability and individual investors.

Kerry Lutz: The dollar, metals prices, and European markets are in such turmoil right now. It's like that old Broadway play, *Stop the World—I Want to Get Off!* But where would anyone go? Fortunately, Martin Armstrong has some ideas. Welcome back, Martin.

Martin Armstrong: Thank you for having me, Kerry.

Kerry Lutz: The dollar seems weak, people say it's heading to the dustbin of history—just not quite yet, right?

Martin Armstrong: Not quite. Honestly, the economic situation is about 25 times worse in Europe than it is here in the U.S. People often focus on the Fed, but if you look closely, Europe's problems are staggering. Bad loans over there have surpassed a trillion dollars, which is why the ECB is even discussing confiscating depositor assets. It's a last-resort measure because European countries can't agree on a unified bailout strategy. For example, Germany doesn't want its taxpayers to foot the bill to save banks in Spain. So, they're talking about putting the burden on depositors.

Kerry Lutz: Confiscating depositor assets? That sounds drastic.

Martin Armstrong: It is. Depositors are now expected to vet their banks, essentially. Europe doesn't have the political unity to organize a massive bailout. Officially, there's around $1.1 trillion in bad loans, but it's probably closer to $1.5 trillion—more than double the $700 billion U.S. bank bailout. It's an unsolvable issue.

Kerry Lutz: Sounds like an intractable crisis.

Martin Armstrong: Exactly. It reminds me of the Savings and Loan (S&L) crisis in the U.S. Congress originally required S&Ls to lend heavily in real estate. Then the rules changed, creating a one-way market where everyone wanted to exit real estate, causing a crash. Congress blamed the S&Ls, but they were just following the rules. In Europe, banks are in a similar situation. They were told to hold sovereign bonds as reserves, thinking they were safe. When Greece defaulted and Cyprus held Greek bonds, it wiped out their banks. It's a sovereign debt crisis, with banks using government debt as reserves— imagine if U.S. states like California or New York went bankrupt. Any bank heavily invested in their bonds would collapse.

Kerry Lutz: So, for Europeans, the best move is to protect their money?

Martin Armstrong: Yes, we're seeing capital flow into the dollar, which is pushing its value up. Right now, the dollar is considered the safest bet, even though Japan's economy is struggling, and Europe is chaotic. The Fed bought around 60% of new U.S. debt last year, while the Bank of England bought close to 100%. The political class isn't solving anything, so these pressures will continue to drive up the dollar, creating a recession in the U.S. by 2016–2020 as the strong dollar hurts American exports.

Kerry Lutz: It sounds like the markets are reacting despite politicians' promises to avoid a currency war.

Martin Armstrong: Exactly. Free markets are effectively checking the politicians, who are often out of their depth. France is proposing something close to communism in Europe, with unified control over money. They've already restricted cash gold transactions, which has killed their bullion market, and buyers have moved to Belgium.

Kerry Lutz: That could lead to unrest. High youth unemployment is already a problem.

Martin Armstrong: Major civil unrest seems inevitable. Youth unemployment is around 60% in some parts of Europe. Many young people no longer believe in socialist promises of taxing the rich. Gallup recently found that 50% of adults in Europe want to migrate to the U.S., and two-thirds of young French citizens want to leave. Countries like Germany and Switzerland are getting overwhelmed by EU immigrants, and the system is fraying at the edges.

Kerry Lutz: If Europe collapses, could Asia be a viable option?

Martin Armstrong: Not yet. Singapore is stable, but even they're seeing some backlash against foreigners. About one-third of work permits aren't being renewed, largely because of inflation. The cost of living there is very high—a two-bedroom apartment costs around $2 million.

Kerry Lutz: Prices are high everywhere. Real estate in Palm Beach County, for example, has seen rising prices driven by foreign buyers.

Martin Armstrong: Yes, high-end properties are in demand as Europeans look to get money out of Europe. Even if they don't see it as a bargain, they view it as a safe place to park funds. It's a diversification strategy, and the U.S. is seen as stable.

Kerry Lutz: Diversification, and maybe a move to low-tax states like Florida to avoid high taxes elsewhere?

Martin Armstrong: Absolutely. People in high-tax states like New York pay around 60% in taxes, whereas Switzerland is about 8.8% and Singapore 15%. The disparity is huge. It's about efficiency too; many lower-tax countries maintain excellent infrastructure with much lower tax rates.

Kerry Lutz: There's also this notion that Washington, D.C. is less focused on the bottom line compared to, say, a private company.

Martin Armstrong: Absolutely. I worked on tax reform in the early '90s, and it was a joke. Politicians could increase revenue with a sales tax over income tax, but they wanted control over individuals. Same with Social Security reform—they wanted to appoint managers, so no real reform happened.

Kerry Lutz: Abolishing the IRS would solve some issues, wouldn't it?

Martin Armstrong: The IRS is the government's most powerful tool for control, especially over the press. Many journalists have told me the government often "asks" them not to cover certain stories. If they don't comply, they get audited. It's selective enforcement.

Kerry Lutz: So, even gold isn't safe in Europe. How do you see metals prices moving?

Martin Armstrong: Gold is likely to bottom around $1,050 to $1,150 by June, with a possible lower low in 2015. We're not seeing a big uptrend until about 2017. Commodities typically surge in short, intense bursts, and I expect a similar move for gold between 2015 and 2017.

Kerry Lutz: That's insightful, Martin. We're excited to see you at the Liberty Mastermind Symposium in Texas this June. We look forward to hearing your perspective on the world economy.

Martin Armstrong: Thank you, Kerry. It's all interconnected—pressure in one area shows up elsewhere.

Kerry Lutz: It really is. For our listeners, check out Martin's regular articles on ArmstrongEconomics.com and join us at the Liberty Mastermind Symposium. Thank you, Martin.

Martin Armstrong: Thank you, Kerry. Looking forward to it.

Key Takeaways:

1. **Currency Instability:** Europe's fragmented fiscal policies are driving depositor asset seizures while the dollar strengthens as a safe haven.
2. **Global Capital Flows:** Capital is moving into the U.S., driving the dollar up, but this creates challenges for American exports and risks recession.
3. **Civil Unrest in Europe:** High unemployment, especially among youth, and increasing taxes are exacerbating social tensions across Europe.
4. **Safe Havens:** Real estate in the U.S. and low-tax jurisdictions are attracting foreign investors seeking to escape financial instability.
5. **Metals Market Outlook:** Gold is expected to bottom by 2015, with significant upward potential by 2017.

Final Thought:

Economic volatility continues to underline the interconnectedness of global financial systems. Understanding these dynamics helps individuals and governments alike navigate crises and plan for a sustainable future.

Debt, Deficits, and the Future of Financial Stability (August 7, 2013)

Interview Summary:

This dialogue between Kerry Lutz and economist Martin Armstrong explores the profound challenges surrounding government debt, deficits, and the broader implications for financial stability. Armstrong delves into historical and contemporary examples to illustrate the risks of fiscal mismanagement, the consequences of perpetual debt, and potential solutions for economic resilience.

Kerry Lutz: Governments actually used to issue annuities because they knew they had no intention of ever paying them back.

Martin Armstrong: Right. They'd essentially say, "You give us $100,000, and we'll pay you interest for the rest of your life. When you pass away, the debt obligation dies with you."

Kerry Lutz: So, like a lottery ticket?

Martin Armstrong: Exactly. And now, it's the same concept with debt—governments just roll it over perpetually. They're essentially annuities that continue indefinitely.

Kerry Lutz: They might as well stop calling them bonds because they're certainly not true bonds anymore.

Martin Armstrong: Agreed. A bond traditionally implies a set period with an obligation to repay. Now, they just roll the debt over, keeping only the interest payments going.

Kerry Lutz: And even if they do return the principal on a 30-year bond, inflation has already eroded its value. A Porsche that cost $50,000 in 1980 now costs nearly $150,000.

Martin Armstrong: Exactly. Investors in long-term government debt almost always lose out to inflation. Governments claim interest rates keep pace with inflation, but they don't. Inflation figures are often skewed in their favor.

Kerry Lutz: In the U.S., we're seeing cities and counties—like Detroit—facing potential defaults with no realistic means to repay their debts. Are we looking at a wave of municipal bankruptcies?

Martin Armstrong: Absolutely. Detroit even defaulted in 1933. We saw similar defaults back in the 1840s. Unfortunately, the people running these governments aren't financial experts. They make promises to get elected and leave the problems for the next administration. The only real solution is to prohibit government borrowing altogether. Live within your means, or don't spend.

Kerry Lutz: The same applies to individuals—you shouldn't borrow to buy things like TVs. Credit used to be limited to things people could realistically afford to repay quickly. Now, it's common to finance daily expenses on credit cards.

Martin Armstrong: Exactly. Credit cards used to require full repayment every month. Then, in 1980, Paul Volcker raised interest rates to 17% to fight inflation, which led to lifting usury laws that capped credit card interest at 6%. Now, we see credit card rates in the 20% range, and they haven't come down since.

Kerry Lutz: And depositors get close to 0.5% interest, while car loans are at 4%.

Martin Armstrong: Precisely. Banks charge high interest on loans while giving virtually nothing on deposits. Banks used to focus on capital allocation to businesses for growth. Now, they're profiting mostly from consumer credit and government debt.

Kerry Lutz: So, for an average person today, if they expect a debt crisis or repudiation, should they take on a mortgage or car loan now if they can service it?

Martin Armstrong: Yes, it's a hedge. If you can lock in a long-term, low-interest rate, go for it. Interest rates are likely to rise significantly.

Kerry Lutz: And that also works as a bet against the dollar?

Martin Armstrong: Exactly. The dollar will likely appreciate due to chaos in Europe, especially if the German elections create uncertainty. We might see the euro fall to 80 cents against the dollar.

Kerry Lutz: So, the U.S. isn't perfect, but it's stable relative to others?

Martin Armstrong: Yes. The U.S. economy has been doing well, though tax increases may slow growth. Europe and Japan are both facing severe challenges. France is targeting major companies like Google and PayPal for taxes, which scares away business. Cities like Detroit face similar issues—taxes keep rising as people leave.

Kerry Lutz: California is facing the same thing—people are moving out, and now they're even imposing exit taxes.

Martin Armstrong: It's absurd. They see citizens as cash cows. Recently, Obama warned that cutting government spending would hurt the economy due to layoffs, but he ignored the fact that tax hikes also take spending power from the private sector.

Kerry Lutz: It's hard to follow their logic. Speaking of debt, "The Debt of Nations" would be a great title for your next book. Adam Smith warned about these issues over 240 years ago in *The Wealth of Nations.*

Martin Armstrong: That's a great title, actually. Smith was spot on. Governments always default on their debt eventually. It's a historical constant.

Kerry Lutz: People can find you at ArmstrongEconomics.com, where you're publishing articles regularly.

Martin Armstrong: Yes, there's a lot happening, and even more to come.

Kerry Lutz: Thanks, Martin. This has been enlightening. We'll check back with you around September for updates on the German elections.

Martin Armstrong: Thanks, Kerry. Take care.

Key Takeaways:

1. **Perpetual Debt Dynamics:** Modern government debt resembles annuities, perpetually rolled over without plans for repayment, leaving future generations with a burden of interest payments.
2. **Inflation and Long-Term Debt:** Inflation erodes the value of long-term bonds, making them a losing proposition for investors despite governments claiming otherwise.
3. **Municipal and Consumer Debt Concerns:** Rising municipal bankruptcies and unchecked consumer credit threaten broader economic stability, necessitating a return to prudent fiscal management.
4. **Strategic Borrowing for Individuals:** Locking in low-interest, long-term loans can hedge against inflation and rising rates, particularly during economic instability.
5. **Tax Policies and Population Migration:** High taxes and policies, such as exit taxes, in states like California and nations like France, drive away residents and businesses, worsening economic challenges.

Final Thought:

The lessons of history—repeated defaults, inflation-driven devaluation, and fiscal irresponsibility—underscore the urgent need for reform in debt and deficit management. Governments, municipalities, and individuals must prioritize sustainable financial practices to ensure future stability. As Armstrong notes, failure to learn from history ensures its repetition.

ECONOMIC SHIFTS, PENSION CRISES, AND THE UNCERTAIN PATH AHEAD (JANUARY 9, 2014)

Interview Summary:

Kerry Lutz talks with Martin Armstrong about the ongoing economic turmoil and what lies ahead for 2014. Armstrong examines the persistent deflationary trends impacting the global economy and addresses the financial crisis faced by European and U.S. pension systems. He explains that many municipal governments, including those in Europe and the U.S., are likely to face bankruptcy due to underfunded pension obligations and rising liabilities—a reality starkly highlighted by Detroit's recent bankruptcy.

Armstrong emphasizes how the old economic model, where individuals could rely on savings, pensions, and stable investments, is now outdated due to inflation-adjusted returns, low-interest rates, and increasing reliance on long-term bonds by pension funds. He highlights that retail investors are notably absent from the stock market, suggesting it has not yet reached bubble levels. According to Armstrong, capital is fleeing to U.S. markets and tangible assets, as investors look for havens in a volatile global landscape. The conversation also touches on the shift toward electronic currency, with Bitcoin positioned as a precursor to digital currencies that may ultimately give governments more control over transactions and reduce tax evasion.

Kerry Lutz: Happy 2014, everyone! Today, we have Martin Armstrong back to discuss what's ahead. Martin, welcome, and Happy New Year!

Martin Armstrong: Happy New Year, Kerry! Thanks for having me.

Kerry Lutz: Let's dive in. 2013 surprised everyone with booming markets, especially stocks. Real estate was strong, too, while gold and commodities didn't perform as expected. How do you see things unfolding?

Martin Armstrong: We're still in a deflationary trend, Kerry. In Europe, things are tough—high youth unemployment, tax hikes, and talk of a potential 10% asset confiscation by the IMF. This is stagflation; assets are inflating, but we're not seeing economic growth to match. In the U.S., there's no massive inflation yet, partly because the Fed's quantitative easing just circulated cash within banks without hitting the broader economy.

Kerry Lutz: It sounds like the effects aren't what people expected. What's happening with pensions?

Martin Armstrong: Pensions are a huge crisis, not just here but in Europe. In Germany, about half the municipal governments could go bankrupt due to unfunded pensions, and Detroit is showing others a possible way out by declaring bankruptcy. Public pensions, which are underfunded, have pushed many municipalities to the brink. In bankruptcy, pensioners will see cuts, with higher earners likely taking the biggest hits.

Kerry Lutz: The traditional retirement model doesn't seem to work anymore. I'm seeing older workers everywhere, filling roles that used to go to younger people.

Martin Armstrong: That's true. People used to think they'd work, save, and retire comfortably, but with interest rates so low, they're not getting returns on their savings. Technology is part of it, too, shifting jobs from traditional roles to companies like Amazon. We're seeing a fundamental shift.

Kerry Lutz: So, is this impacting the markets?

Martin Armstrong: Yes, in several ways. The stock market isn't in a bubble like 2007. Retail investors are largely absent. Instead, capital is fleeing to the U.S. from Europe due to fears of asset confiscation. Even pension funds are moving back into equities because they can't survive on bonds at today's rates.

Kerry Lutz: And what about insurance companies? They're also struggling with low returns.

Martin Armstrong: Absolutely. Insurance companies, like pensions, need high returns to pay out on annuities and life insurance. But with bond yields down, they face the same problem. This all stems from the aging population driving up demand for long-term bonds, which lowered yields.

Kerry Lutz: With lower yields, are we moving toward more private investment?

Martin Armstrong: Exactly. People will flock to private assets—real estate, stocks, precious metals, and commodities. We're already seeing a shift toward private sector investments because the government sector is in trouble. This shift in thinking will become more evident as more municipal defaults happen in Europe and beyond.

Kerry Lutz: You've mentioned electronic currency before. Do you think Bitcoin is leading us there?

Martin Armstrong: Bitcoin is interesting, but I see it more as a stepping stone toward government-controlled electronic currencies. Governments aim to eliminate cash to prevent tax evasion. The electronic currency push is gaining traction globally, and Bitcoin is helping to acclimate people to this shift.

Kerry Lutz: And if we see more defaults, won't people lose faith in government debt?

Martin Armstrong: Absolutely. We're likely to see a flight to private sector assets as faith in government bonds declines. The public-private investment shift will redefine what people see as a safe haven. When government becomes the problem, people look elsewhere.

Kerry Lutz: You're right about that. Thank you, Martin! For those interested in learning more, visit ArmstrongEconomics.com. We're also holding the Liberty Mastermind Symposium in Las Vegas this February. It's a fantastic event where you can learn from top minds on how to navigate these turbulent times. Thanks again, Martin!

Martin Armstrong: Thanks, Kerry! Happy New Year, and best of luck navigating the year ahead.

Key Takeaways:

1. **Pension Crises:** Underfunded pensions threaten municipal bankruptcies in Europe and the U.S., with Detroit's example showing the likely outcomes for pensioners.
2. **Deflationary Trends:** The global economy is in a deflationary phase, with stagnant growth and financial strain on both governments and individuals.
3. **Shifts to Private Assets:** As government bonds and pensions become less reliable, capital is moving into private investments like stocks, real estate, and precious metals.
4. **Rise of Electronic Currency:** Bitcoin and similar technologies are precursors to government-backed digital currencies aimed at reducing tax evasion and increasing transaction control.
5. **Economic Realignment:** Faith in government debt is eroding, prompting investors to seek stability in tangible assets and private sector opportunities.

Final Thought:

As economic challenges persist, focusing on private investments and tangible assets while staying alert to shifts in global finance and technology will be crucial for navigating the uncertain path ahead.

STOCK MARKET, SOVEREIGN DEBT, AND GLOBAL POLICY IMPACTS (JUNE 3, 2014)

Interview Summary:

In June 2014, Martin Armstrong discusses pressing economic issues with Kerry Lutz. Armstrong maintains his forecast that the stock market could significantly rise, fueled by forced investments from pension funds and declining interest rates. He explains that the current market momentum is driven by necessity rather than retail speculation, with pension funds seeking alternatives to low-yield bonds, thereby pushing money into equities.

Armstrong also warns of a looming "sovereign debt crisis" similar to the 1931 defaults, which could start in Europe and possibly involve countries like France and Greece. The conversation covers the impacts of falling bond yields, with long-term rates driven down by institutional demand rather than Federal Reserve manipulation. This phenomenon, Armstrong explains, is partly a result of an aging population seeking secure returns, forcing pension funds to chase bonds and, subsequently, equities as interest rates edge toward zero or even negative.

Further, Armstrong discusses the implications of global capital flows on the dollar and U.S. equities. As other economies weaken, the U.S. attracts foreign institutional capital due to its relatively stable economic environment, despite ongoing government regulatory constraints like FATCA, which he argues has created obstacles for Americans abroad and restricted global business operations.

The conversation also touches on the role of commodities, with Armstrong predicting a potential rise in commodity prices post-2016. He criticizes recent geopolitical conflicts as financially motivated rather than ideological, citing examples like the Syrian conflict, which

59

he attributes to competition over energy pipelines. Additionally, Armstrong expresses skepticism about gold as a hedge, suggesting that it may still be in a bearish phase until it reaches a significant low.

Armstrong concludes with thoughts on societal instability driven by government overreach and unsustainable pension liabilities. He foresees potential civil unrest as governments struggle to meet obligations. He suggests that separatist movements and increased civil dissent could emerge as people seek alternatives to government policies, warning that these economic and social dynamics are set to intensify in the coming years.

Kerry Lutz: So, Martin, what's going on with the stock market? Are you sticking to your forecast that it might go up substantially, maybe even double?

Martin Armstrong: Yes, that's still my expectation. Markets tend to swing to extremes. Right now, what we're seeing isn't a traditional bullish market driven by retail excitement. Instead, a lot of people, especially institutional players like pension funds, are being forced into the market because interest rates are so low. We're even talking about negative interest rates now.

Kerry Lutz: So, pension funds are driving this?

Martin Armstrong: Exactly. These funds were originally designed assuming returns around 8%. With rates so low, they've had to look elsewhere, even getting into equities. But it's quality stocks with dividends that are seeing the action, not speculative stocks. And then, in Europe, there's a lot of fear about asset confiscation. There was a recent leak that the European Central Bank might want a 10% tax on all deposits, which has spooked people further.

Kerry Lutz: What about bonds? The 10-year is down to around 2.5%. What's that telling you?

Martin Armstrong: That drop reflects concerns about negative rates and the sheer demand from pension funds looking for guaranteed returns. The Federal Reserve can control short-term rates but not the long end. Most of this demand for long-term bonds is from pension funds aiming to lock in income. That's what's driven rates down.

Kerry Lutz: So, is the economy heading for more of the same slow or even negative growth?

Martin Armstrong: In most places, yes. The U.S. is showing some growth, but it's marginal. Global trade accounts for about 60% of world GDP, but real growth is low. There's a lot of big money flowing into U.S. assets because, globally, there aren't many safe places left. Europe has credit risks country-by-country, Japan is struggling, and China recently struggled to sell its bonds.

Kerry Lutz: The Treasury recently announced that 77,000 global banks will report on any American clients abroad. How's that affecting things?

Martin Armstrong: It's actually hurting the world economy because it discourages business with Americans abroad. I know people who can't open accounts due to these regulations. Americans living overseas have been refused banking services entirely.

Kerry Lutz: Switching to commodities—what do you see for oil and gas prices?

Martin Armstrong: Commodities may rise post-2016, as we're seeing moves by governments that impact the market. The conflict in Syria, for instance, is more about pipeline routes than ideology, with countries vying to control gas supplies to Europe. These geopolitical conflicts are often tied to trade and energy.

Kerry Lutz: And what about gold?

Martin Armstrong: Gold, unlike equities, doesn't provide an income, so it's less attractive to institutions. If gold closes below $1,190 monthly, it might drop below $1,000. We could see a low around $900, which would set it up to move higher later.

Kerry Lutz: Let's discuss derivatives. Are they as dangerous as some claim?

Martin Armstrong: Derivatives serve a purpose, like hedging currency risks. However, certain types, such as those tied to mortgage-backed securities, were risky. When Greece defaulted, people who held risk contracts didn't get paid. So, some derivatives are essentially gambling, especially with the way banks define default.

Kerry Lutz: Are we heading for a sovereign debt crisis?

Martin Armstrong: That's a real possibility. In 1931, the crisis wasn't about stocks but rather sovereign debt defaults. Several countries, including Austria and Germany, defaulted, causing contagion. If today's debt crisis hits, especially with these high levels of government debt, we could see defaults worldwide.

Kerry Lutz: Are we likely to see unrest as governments struggle with debt?

Martin Armstrong: Yes. In Europe, we're already seeing separatist movements, like Scotland's vote to leave the U.K. This trend may grow as people become more frustrated with government overreach, unfunded pension liabilities, and rising taxes. It's a worrying trend, and it's why people are increasingly looking for alternatives.

Kerry Lutz: So, do you think people are looking for some kind of safe haven, especially with the governments clamping down on money movement?

Martin Armstrong: Yes, but the reality is, there aren't many options left. We used to hear about ways people could leave with assets, like in

Russia with gold sewn into clothing or hidden in luggage. But today, with metal detectors and tighter controls, it's incredibly hard to move wealth privately. People are feeling trapped, and with governments closing off more options, there's a growing sense of frustration.

Key Takeaways:

1. **Stock Market Growth:** Institutional investments, especially from pension funds, are driving stock markets higher, despite concerns of negative interest rates.
2. **Sovereign Debt Risks:** Europe is at risk of sovereign debt defaults, reminiscent of the 1931 crisis, with potential contagion across markets.
3. **Capital Flight:** Global capital is flowing into U.S. assets due to perceived safety, though regulatory hurdles like FATCA are limiting Americans' international options.
4. **Commodities and Gold:** Commodities may rise post-2016, while gold remains bearish in the near term, with a potential low of $900 before recovery.
5. **Civil Unrest:** Rising taxes, unfunded pensions, and government overreach are fueling separatist movements and growing societal discontent globally.

Final Thought:

Martin Armstrong emphasizes the need for vigilance and adaptability in the face of mounting economic, social, and geopolitical challenges. Understanding these trends can help individuals make informed decisions to safeguard their financial futures in increasingly uncertain times, through 2017.

CYCLES OF WEALTH, MARKETS, AND POWER: ANALYZING THE GLOBAL ECONOMIC LANDSCAPE (JULY 25, 2014)

Interview Summary:

Martin Armstrong provides a detailed analysis of the economic and financial landscape in 2014, emphasizing the interplay between market cycles, government debt, and the behavior of global capital. The conversation explores the ongoing resilience of the U.S. stock market, the pressures facing global currencies, and the looming shifts toward electronic money. Armstrong underscores the inevitability of economic cycles and the challenges posed by centralized authority and regulatory overreach.

Kerry Lutz: Welcome back to *The Financial Survival Network*! We have Martin Armstrong here to discuss the stock market, the world economy, and the dollar. Martin, always a pleasure to have you.

Martin Armstrong: Thank you for inviting me. Always great to be here.

Kerry Lutz: Everyone is predicting a stock market crash any day now. There's a lot of anxiety about where to put money, given the lack of alternatives. You've been consistently saying the market will go higher. Has anything changed?

Martin Armstrong: Not at all. The market has been steadily climbing in a methodical manner—not in a bubble-like frenzy yet. Short term, there may be minor corrections, but overall, the trend remains upward.

When you look globally, the question is: where else would major institutions put their money?

For individuals, buying gold is an option, but institutions can't. As for currencies, the U.S. dollar stands out despite our $17 trillion debt. That debt gives depth to the market, meaning there's room to park substantial funds. Pension funds and trillion-dollar portfolios simply don't have better alternatives than the dollar.

Kerry Lutz: So what's driving the dollar's dominance?

Martin Armstrong: The euro eliminated individual currencies in Europe, but the credit quality varies widely—Greece and Germany both use euros, but they're worlds apart economically. Other currencies like the yuan, pesos, or rubles don't have the depth or reliability for serious investment.

Despite criticisms, the dollar is the go-to currency. The European Central Bank (ECB) is moving toward negative interest rates and flooding the market with euros to counteract their economic stagnation. Taxes in Europe are so high—over 50% for the average German—that new businesses can't even get started. Meanwhile, unemployment among European youth exceeds 60%. The dollar benefits because capital flows away from those challenges.

Kerry Lutz: You mentioned a coordinated move by central banks. What's happening there?

Martin Armstrong: There's a secret agreement among central banks: the U.S., New Zealand, Australia, Canada, and Britain will raise interest rates while Europe lowers theirs. The goal is to redirect some capital back to Europe, but it won't work. Europe's banking crisis is severe, and the International Monetary Fund (IMF) has floated the idea of confiscating 10% of all bank deposits. When they tried this in Cyprus, depositors lost closer to 50%.

Kerry Lutz: That's alarming. How are people reacting?

Martin Armstrong: Europeans are pulling their money out of banks and investing in real estate, particularly in New York and Florida. Canadians, too, are buying U.S. property because Canada has announced similar "bail-in" plans. Chinese buyers dominate the high-end market, but Canadians are now the largest buyers of U.S. properties by volume.

Kerry Lutz: What about China? They're encouraging property purchases abroad.

Martin Armstrong: China understands cycles better than the West. Their approach aligns with their cultural acceptance of cyclical activity, unlike the West, which tries to "fix" cycles through interventions. This is why China has been booming—it embraces the natural rhythm of economic activity.

Kerry Lutz: So what's the role of central banks in all of this?

Martin Armstrong: Central banks react to cycles rather than control them. Contrary to popular belief, stock markets rise with interest rates and fall when rates decline. Historical data supports this. For example, interest rates peaked at 6% in 1929 and fell to 1% during the Great Depression, but that didn't save the market. Japan's experience with low rates for decades also shows that interest rates aren't the sole driver of economic cycles.

Kerry Lutz: So where does the blame lie?

Martin Armstrong: Congress is the real problem. The $17 trillion national debt is largely cumulative interest. Congress borrows endlessly without ever paying down the principal. It's a Ponzi scheme disguised as governance. The Fed often gets scapegoated, but it can't neutralize the fiscal irresponsibility of Congress.

Kerry Lutz: How does this end?

Martin Armstrong: Historically, no one escapes the cycle. Confidence eventually breaks, and debt becomes unsellable. We're already seeing signs of this—China, Russia, and even the U.S. have had trouble selling bonds. In Europe, the ECB steps in to buy unsold sovereign debt. Once confidence collapses, the system crashes, forcing a reset.

Kerry Lutz: The euro seems especially vulnerable.

Martin Armstrong: The euro was flawed from the start. Its creators knew it couldn't work but assumed they could "fix" it later. Now, their solution is to demand more power for Brussels and strip member countries of sovereignty. This will only exacerbate Europe's problems.

Kerry Lutz: You've mentioned cycles frequently. Can we prepare for them?

Martin Armstrong: Cycles can't be stopped, but you can prepare. Like Joseph in the Bible advising Pharaoh, you stockpile resources during good years to mitigate the impact of the bad years. However, governments often try to stop downturns entirely, which is impossible.

Kerry Lutz: What about electronic currency? Is that part of the future?

Martin Armstrong: Absolutely. We're moving toward a cashless society. Countries like Canada are already issuing plastic currency, and many European cities are transitioning to cashless transactions. Governments prefer this because it eliminates tax evasion and prevents bank runs.

Kerry Lutz: So, where does gold fit into this future?

Martin Armstrong: Gold will become a refuge for those seeking to escape the system. However, the move to electronic money will make gold harder to use in transactions. Its value will be less about inflation hedging and more about staying "off the grid."

Kerry Lutz: Final thoughts on the current state of the world?

Martin Armstrong: We're in a late-stage cycle where taxes will rise dramatically, and economic hardship will worsen through 2020. Social unrest and war cycles are intensifying. Governments will continue to seek more power, but they can't escape the inevitable corrections of history.

Kerry Lutz: As always, insightful analysis, Martin. Where can listeners find more of your work?

Martin Armstrong: Visit *ArmstrongEconomics.com* for more insights. We'll also have a new report on gold out soon.

Kerry Lutz: Thanks, Martin. Always a pleasure.

Martin Armstrong: Thank you, Kerry.

Key Takeaways:

1. **Stock Market Outlook:** The market is steadily climbing, driven by the lack of viable alternatives for institutional capital.
2. **Dollar Dominance:** The U.S. dollar remains the world's reserve currency due to its depth and reliability despite high national debt.
3. **Debt Crisis Looms:** Global confidence in sovereign debt is eroding, signaling an eventual crash and systemic reset.
4. **Rise of Electronic Currency:** Governments are moving toward cashless systems to enhance tax collection and eliminate bank runs.
5. **Gold's Role:** Gold will serve as a hedge against government control in a cashless future.
6. **The Power of Cycles:** Economic, social, and political cycles are inevitable, but preparation can mitigate their impact.

Final Thought:

The current global economic landscape is shaped by the inevitable cycles of history, with rising debt, centralized power, and shifting capital flows signaling transformative changes ahead. As governments push toward cashless systems and tighter controls, gold and other tangible assets will serve as key refuges. Understanding and preparing for these cycles is essential to navigate the challenges of a rapidly evolving world.

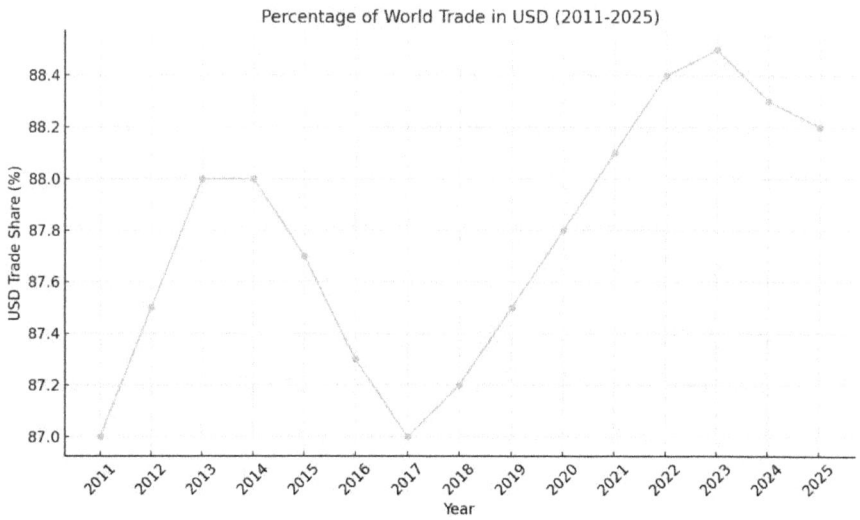

Percentage of World Trade in USD (2011-2025)

THE SHIFTING SANDS OF GLOBAL CAPITAL AND CONFIDENCE (AUGUST 27, 2014)

Interview Summary:

In this illuminating discussion, Martin Armstrong delves into the dynamics of global capital flows, the implications of declining confidence in government, and his forecasts for the stock market, precious metals, and global economies. With his Economic Confidence Model as the foundation, Armstrong highlights the interconnectedness of global markets and the inevitable cycles of economic bubbles.

Armstrong argues that the U.S. stock market's rise is driven by massive capital inflows from regions with weaker economic prospects, such as Europe. These inflows stem from the lack of viable alternatives for global institutional investors. He critiques the misconceptions of retail investors and mainstream analysts, emphasizing that current conditions are not indicative of a bubble but rather a response to geopolitical instability and economic mismanagement abroad.

Addressing government debt, Armstrong predicts a sovereign debt crisis that will initially impact Europe but eventually spread globally. He explains how public mistrust in government will lead to significant shifts in financial capital, with private assets like real estate, equities, and eventually gold becoming safe havens. He underscores that gold is not a hedge against inflation but a hedge against government instability.

Armstrong also touches on the broader consequences of governments seeking to eliminate cash, the rise of electronic currencies, and the dangers of unchecked taxation. He warns of the global implications of excessive government spending, particularly the militarization of economies like the U.S., which he compares to the fall of the Roman Empire.

71

Kerry Lutz: If you haven't heard Martin Armstrong before, you need to listen to him now. Martin, the forecaster's forecaster, has been right, while others have been wrong about the stock market. The Dow is over 17,000; the S&P 500 is over 2,000—exactly as you predicted. Martin, welcome back.

Martin Armstrong: Thanks for having me.

Kerry Lutz: So, with markets at these levels, I'm guessing you're not surprised?

Martin Armstrong: Not at all. People need to understand that most analysis is too domestically focused. We're in a global capital flow cycle, and right now, there's no better alternative than the U.S. dollar and U.S. equities. Europe is a mess—the euro is failing, France just fired its entire government, and countries like Britain and Canada don't have economies large enough to absorb global capital.

Kerry Lutz: So, is it just by default that the U.S. is benefiting?

Martin Armstrong: Precisely. Capital has to go somewhere. You're not going to put it in Russian rubles or Chinese yuan. The dollar is still the safest option. Central banks, unable to diversify further, are even buying equities. Countries like Switzerland are trying to spread risk into currencies like the Canadian and Australian dollars, but the majority is still flowing into U.S. assets.

Kerry Lutz: You've written about margin debt as well. Some analysts point to it as a sign of a bubble. What's your take?

Martin Armstrong: It's a misunderstanding. Retail investors aren't driving this market, and margin debt isn't speculative in nature. Low interest rates make borrowing attractive, and many investors are earning better returns from dividends than bonds. This isn't like the frothy bubble of 2000—it's fundamentally different.

Kerry Lutz: For a retail investor with $10,000 to $15,000, how do you recommend playing this market?

Martin Armstrong: Look for dips. The S&P 500 is likely heading toward the 3,000 range. The broader market is benefiting from institutional capital flows, but the key is understanding these cycles and taking advantage of corrections.

Kerry Lutz: You've said the U.S. isn't far behind Europe in terms of municipal debt issues. Can you elaborate?

Martin Armstrong: The fundamental issue is that governments have promised pensions without funding them. Municipalities, like Detroit, are collapsing because they're paying for retirees while still needing to hire new workers. The cost of government is rising exponentially, and the system is unsustainable.

Kerry Lutz: What about government attempts to transition to electronic currencies?

Martin Armstrong: This is a long-term goal. Governments want to eliminate cash to collect every tax dollar and control the economy more directly. Electronic currencies give them this power. In Europe, cash withdrawals are increasingly restricted. These trends will only intensify.

Kerry Lutz: Speaking of control, what about gold and its role in a portfolio?

Martin Armstrong: Gold isn't a hedge against inflation—it's a hedge against government instability. It rises when confidence in government collapses. That's why we saw it peak during the 2008 crisis. I expect gold to rise again in 2016 as sovereign debt issues worsen.

Kerry Lutz: And you see a new currency system emerging eventually?

Martin Armstrong: Historically, that's always the outcome. Governments reset their systems when debts become unmanageable. We're heading toward a shift to electronic currencies and possibly new reserve systems.

Kerry Lutz: You've often discussed the shift of financial power from West to East. How is China positioned?

Martin Armstrong: China is unique. Unlike Russia, which destroyed individual enterprise under communism, China allowed family bonds and entrepreneurship to survive. While they're not entirely confident in their government, the people are more self-reliant. This is why China has grown rapidly, unlike Russia, which remains stagnant.

Kerry Lutz: And yet, much of China's wealth is leaving the country. Why?

Martin Armstrong: It's about self-preservation. Wealthy individuals understand the risks of government control and seek safer havens. That's why we're seeing Chinese buyers dominate high-end U.S. real estate markets.

Kerry Lutz: Your Economic Confidence Model has been remarkably accurate. Can you explain how it works?

Martin Armstrong: The model tracks global capital flows and cycles of speculation. Every 8.6 years, there's a major bubble—whether in commodities, real estate, or stocks. These cycles are driven by human nature, and by analyzing them collectively, we can predict the broader trends.

Kerry Lutz: Fascinating. Any final thoughts?

Martin Armstrong: The key is understanding that we're all connected. Sovereign debt issues in Europe will impact the U.S. and Asia. Confidence in government is the linchpin—once it erodes, capital will flee to private assets, driving up their value.

Kerry Lutz: Thanks, Martin. For more insights, visit ArmstrongEconomics.com and subscribe to Martin's newsletter.

Martin Armstrong: Thanks, Kerry. It's always a pleasure.

Key Takeaways:

1. **Stock Market Dynamics:** Capital flows from unstable regions are driving U.S. equity markets higher, with the S&P 500 poised for further gains.
2. **Government Debt Issues:** Unfunded pensions and rising costs are leading to municipal bankruptcies, mirroring Europe's sovereign debt crisis.
3. **Gold's Role:** Gold serves as a hedge against government instability, not inflation, and will rise when public confidence collapses.
4. **The End of Cash:** Governments are moving toward electronic currencies to enhance control and taxation, marking a significant shift in the global financial system.
5. **Global Economic Cycles:** Human nature drives cycles of speculation, with bubbles forming approximately every 8.6 years. Understanding these patterns is key to navigating markets.

Final Thought:

The global economy is undergoing a transformation fueled by sovereign debt crises, shifting capital, and declining trust in governments. As instability grows and traditional systems falter, private assets like equities, real estate, and gold will become key safe havens. Confidence in government is the tipping point—its erosion will drive a shift toward tangible assets, innovation, and systemic resets, reshaping the global financial landscape.

The Rise and Fall of Governments and Financial Systems (December 14, 2014)

Interview Summary:

Martin Armstrong discusses a range of topics with Kerry Lutz, including the release of his documentary *The Forecaster*, systemic failures in government, and looming economic challenges. Armstrong shares personal insights into his experiences with the judicial system, highlighting how corporations are denied constitutional rights, leaving corporate officers vulnerable to legal abuse. He critiques the erosion of due process and the rise of government overreach, calling the current state of governance in the U.S. and globally "totalitarian."

Armstrong delves into cycles of government oppression, economic mismanagement, and social discontent, arguing that these patterns repeat throughout history. He notes how rising taxes and unfunded pension obligations are collapsing governments worldwide, similar to the decline of Rome. He warns that sovereign debt crises, particularly in Europe, will trigger widespread contagion, destabilizing global economies.

The conversation shifts to markets, where Armstrong predicts continued deflation and a rise in tangible assets like stocks, art, and real estate. He sees the stock market as a safe haven amid sovereign debt instability and anticipates a paradigm shift in energy, with solar and natural gas leading the way. He also discusses cultural and economic changes, such as the influx of foreign investment in U.S. real estate and China's challenges with wealth flight.

Finally, Armstrong emphasizes the importance of understanding historical cycles to navigate present challenges while urging significant political and economic reforms to address systemic failures.

Kerry Lutz: Welcome to *The Financial Survival Network*. It's December 14, 2014. We're excited to have Martin Armstrong with us. Martin, congratulations on the release of *The Forecaster*. You're going to be an international celebrity—whether you like it or not.

Martin Armstrong: We'll see about that. Becoming a celebrity was never one of my goals.

Kerry Lutz: Your story is compelling—you're like "the man who knew too much." You've faced incredible challenges, and now the truth might finally come out. How do you feel about that?

Martin Armstrong: The judicial system in the U.S. is not what people think. We're told about due process and constitutional rights, but that's largely fiction. In my case, the government used a legal loophole, claiming I was a corporate officer and corporations have no constitutional rights. That's how they bypassed the Fifth Amendment to hold me in contempt.

Kerry Lutz: So corporations have no rights, and their officers lose theirs too?

Martin Armstrong: Exactly. It's a dangerous precedent. The Constitution is meant to be a restraint on government, not a tool for it to do whatever it wants. But courts have flipped this, giving government unchecked power. For example, Obama asked the FCC to regulate the internet without involving Congress. Now we have to prove we have a right not to be regulated—it's completely backward.

Kerry Lutz: That's alarming. Judges and prosecutors seem to wield unchecked power.

Martin Armstrong: Absolutely. Take grand juries—they're one-sided. Prosecutors don't have to present exculpatory evidence, only facts that support their case. Most cases never make it to trial because the system pressures people to accept plea deals. If you go to trial, you risk much harsher sentences.

Kerry Lutz: That's the carrot-and-stick approach—plead guilty and get a lighter sentence. It's coercive.

Martin Armstrong: It's worse than that. Public defenders are often overwhelmed, and defendants can't afford to fight. This is why plea bargains dominate, and justice rarely gets served.

Kerry Lutz: How does this tie into cycles of government and public sentiment?

Martin Armstrong: We're in a cycle of oppressive government and declining public trust. Governments are collapsing under unfunded pensions and rising taxes. People are fed up. Socialism is failing because it's unsustainable. Rome faced the same issue—its pension system collapsed, leading to the empire's decline.

Kerry Lutz: History repeating itself?

Martin Armstrong: Exactly. Governments always assume they can tax their way out of problems, but there's a breaking point. In Europe, youth unemployment exceeds 60% in some areas because high taxes discourage small businesses. The system is imploding.

Kerry Lutz: And education seems to be part of the problem—students graduate with massive debt and limited job prospects.

Martin Armstrong: Education in its current form is a fraud. Colleges push degrees as essential, yet most graduates don't work in their field of study. Forbes reported that 65% of college graduates end up in jobs that don't require a degree.

Kerry Lutz: And economic statistics are often manipulated to suit political narratives.

Martin Armstrong: Absolutely. Economic data is designed to fit political agendas, not reflect reality. For example, trade deficits don't account for currency fluctuations, making the data meaningless. Policymakers use this flawed data to justify harmful regulations.

Kerry Lutz: Speaking of flawed policies, let's talk about Europe and the Swiss referendum on gold.

Martin Armstrong: The Swiss system allows referendums if enough signatures are gathered. While the gold referendum aimed to limit the Swiss National Bank's ability to sell reserves, its failure would likely embolden the bank to liquidate more gold.

Kerry Lutz: What about Europe's broader economic issues?

Martin Armstrong: The euro is fundamentally flawed because it unified currencies without unifying debt. Each country retains its own debt, creating imbalances. It's like the U.S. using state debt as reserves instead of federal debt—it's unsustainable. Once one European country defaults, contagion will spread across the region.

Kerry Lutz: And how does this impact the U.S. stock market?

Martin Armstrong: Capital flight will drive U.S. markets higher as global instability worsens. While there will be fluctuations, the Dow could reach 23,000 to 26,000, possibly higher if sovereign debt crises escalate. The stock market remains the safest place for institutional capital.

Kerry Lutz: What about real estate?

Martin Armstrong: High-end real estate is booming as foreign investors seek safe havens. Miami and New York are prime examples. However, middle-tier real estate could face challenges as governments tighten credit and enforce stricter regulations.

Kerry Lutz: How do you see energy markets evolving?

Martin Armstrong: Oil's decline reflects a broader paradigm shift. Renewable energy, particularly solar, is becoming more viable and will eventually displace coal. Electric vehicles are also reducing demand for oil. The Middle East's influence is waning, and energy costs should continue to decline.

Kerry Lutz: So, the world is changing rapidly, but governments seem incapable of adapting.

Martin Armstrong: That's the core issue—governments refuse to reform. Politicians borrow endlessly, assuming debts will never need repayment. This mindset is delusional and will ultimately lead to sovereign defaults.

Kerry Lutz: Martin, thanks for your insights. For listeners, check out *The Forecaster* and visit ArmstrongEconomics.com to stay informed.

Martin Armstrong: Thanks, Kerry. It's better to understand what's happening and prepare than to be caught off guard.

Key Insights:

1. Governments globally are collapsing under the weight of unfunded pensions, rising taxes, and debt mismanagement.
2. Sovereign debt crises in Europe will trigger contagion, destabilizing economies worldwide.
3. The U.S. stock market will benefit from capital flight, while high-end real estate remains a safe haven for international investors.
4. Renewable energy and technological innovation are reshaping global markets, reducing dependence on oil.

5. Fundamental political and economic reforms are needed to address systemic failures, but history suggests resistance to change is the norm.

Final Thought:

Understanding historical cycles is crucial to navigating present challenges as systemic failures in governance and economics continue to shape global realities.

The Collapse of Trust: Swiss Peg Break and Global Economic Strain (January 20, 2015)

Interview Summary:

In this dialogue, Martin Armstrong dissects the economic and political chaos triggered by the Swiss National Bank's decision to abandon its peg to the euro, marking a pivotal moment in global markets. The conversation explores the broader implications of sovereign debt, flawed monetary systems, and government overreach. Armstrong predicts escalating instability in Europe and warns that the global economic structure is on a collision course with reality.

Kerry Lutz: The world seems to be going crazy. To help us make sense of it, we have Martin Armstrong. Martin, welcome back!

Martin Armstrong: Thanks for having me.

Kerry Lutz: The Swiss National Bank dropped its peg to the euro, and chaos seems to be reigning. Precious metals are finally climbing. What's going on, and what can we expect?

Martin Armstrong: I've received a lot of emails congratulating me on calling the gold pop, but it's important to understand why this is happening. Gold isn't rising due to inflation or quantitative easing—it's a hedge against government. This move stems largely from Europe, not the U.S., and it began with the Swiss peg collapse.

The euro is the root problem. It's a disaster. Politicians and bureaucrats in Brussels are focused on their own survival, not what's best for Europe. Instead of reforming the system and admitting their mistakes, they're doubling down by buying sovereign debt. I've told clients: sell everything to them. You've got a buyer—let them have it. It's a joke.

Kerry Lutz: What's driving this massive bond-buying spree?

Martin Armstrong: It's fear. Germany's 10-year interest rate is at 0.4%, while Greece is over 9%. In the U.S., our 10-year rate is about 1.8%, which is higher than Germany's. But Germany's economy is in worse shape than the U.S. People are buying German bonds, betting that when the euro cracks, they'll get Deutsche marks. There's zero confidence in Europe, and this mirrors the capital flight we saw in 1931.

Kerry Lutz: So we're witnessing a repeat of history?

Martin Armstrong: Absolutely. The capital flows are coming to the U.S., pushing the dollar higher. That, in turn, will break other pegs. It's chaos, pure chaos. And the root cause is systemic: we keep electing academics and lawyers who don't understand economics. They write laws, but they don't grasp the broader consequences.

Kerry Lutz: You've written about the impact of failing pensions. What happens when these pensions go bust?

Martin Armstrong: It's a ticking time bomb. Municipalities never properly funded pensions. They assumed they could always raise taxes to cover the gap. Now, retired workers still need to be paid, and replacements have to be hired, doubling the cost of government. This is why Detroit failed—nearly 60% of its revenue went to pensions, leaving no money for current expenses.

This same trend is happening everywhere. Property taxes will keep rising, and people who can't afford them will lose their homes. It's a broken system. Property taxes, in particular, are an injustice—you never truly own your home.

Kerry Lutz: So where does this lead?

Martin Armstrong: We're heading for a crash-and-burn scenario. Unfortunately, meaningful reform only comes after a crisis. Look at 1933: the U.S. got FDR, Germany got Hitler, and China got Mao. When things collapse, people throw out whoever is in power. In our case, the Republicans will likely get blamed, setting the stage for a major political shift in 2016.

Kerry Lutz: Your models project a rise in third-party activity. How does that factor into this?

Martin Armstrong: Yes, 2016 will see a significant spike in third-party sentiment. People are realizing that both major parties are the same when it comes to economic issues. The Republican Party might even split, with traditional "country club" Republicans diverging from the populist base.

Kerry Lutz: For the average person, how should they prepare?

Martin Armstrong: Diversify. Hold some gold, but stick to coins, not bars, to avoid tracking. Keep a stockpile of cash, as banks—particularly major ones in New York—will be hit hard during the downturn. Focus on private sector investments, as public sector debt is becoming increasingly toxic.

Kerry Lutz: What about the stock market?

Martin Armstrong: The stock market is consolidating, but the bond market is in a massive bubble. Pension funds in the U.S. have about 40% in bonds, while in Europe, some funds are mandated to hold 80% in sovereign debt. This will end disastrously. When the bond bubble bursts, capital will shift to equities and corporate bonds.

Kerry Lutz: You've also spoken about global reliance on the U.S. dollar. How does that play into this?

Martin Armstrong: The dollar's dominance is a double-edged sword. Emerging markets have issued $6 trillion in dollar-denominated debt since 2007, thinking it was safe. But as the dollar appreciates, these debts become unpayable. This dynamic is strip-mining emerging markets of their wealth.

Kerry Lutz: It sounds bleak. Is there any hope for leadership to step in and fix this?

Martin Armstrong: Not beforehand. Our political system is too dysfunctional. Politicians only act when faced with catastrophe, and even then, they often make the wrong decisions.

Kerry Lutz: You've also mentioned a shift in financial hubs. What's happening there?

Martin Armstrong: Wall Street is migrating out of New York. Goldman Sachs is already across the river in New Jersey, and others are following. High taxes and real estate costs are driving them out. Florida, with its lack of state income tax, is becoming a major hub for hedge funds and financial firms.

Kerry Lutz: You've been following the response to *The Forecaster*. How's it doing?

Martin Armstrong: It's been incredibly well-received in Europe and will debut in Germany in April. There's even talk of a global pay-per-view event due to demand from the financial industry. The film is sparking conversations about financial corruption and systemic issues, which is encouraging.

Kerry Lutz: Thanks for your time, Martin. As always, people can find your insights at ArmstrongEconomics.com.

Martin Armstrong: Thank you, Kerry. It's always a pleasure.

Key Takeaways:

1. **Swiss Peg Collapse:** The abandonment of the Swiss franc peg to the euro marks a turning point in global confidence in European monetary policy.
2. **Pensions Under Siege:** Unfunded pensions are straining municipalities, leading to rising taxes and inevitable defaults.
3. **Bond Market Bubble:** With interest rates at historic lows, the bond market is unsustainable and poised for collapse.
4. **The Dollar's Dominance:** The U.S. dollar's strength is destabilizing emerging markets that issued dollar-denominated debt.
5. **Migration of Financial Hubs:** High-tax states like New York are losing financial institutions to more business-friendly states like Florida.
6. **Political Shifts:** Growing dissatisfaction with traditional parties could lead to a major realignment in U.S. politics by 2016.

Final Thought:

The Swiss peg collapse underscores a growing global mistrust in monetary systems and government policies. With pensions faltering, a bond market bubble nearing its limit, and political dissatisfaction rising, systemic reform seems inevitable—but only after crisis strikes. In the meantime, diversifying assets and understanding shifting financial dynamics will be crucial for navigating these turbulent times.

THE FORECASTER, GLOBAL TURMOIL, AND ECONOMIC REALITIES (MARCH 10, 2015)

Interview Summary:

Kerry Lutz welcomes Martin Armstrong to discuss the release of *The Forecaster,* a documentary about Armstrong's life and work. They delve into the challenges of distributing the film in the U.S. due to corporate and governmental pressures, highlighting issues of censorship in media. Armstrong shares personal experiences with government surveillance, hacking, and interference, emphasizing the erosion of privacy and free press globally.

The conversation shifts to economic topics, including the trajectory of the U.S. stock market, the decline of the euro, and the rise of the dollar. Armstrong explains that the euro is a failing currency and predicts further drops against the dollar. They explore the systemic flaws in Europe's banking system, exacerbated by government bonds that aren't marked to market. Armstrong also criticizes modern education systems and advocates for the effectiveness of apprenticeship models.

The discussion concludes with insights on gold's decline, the impact of a strengthening dollar, and the long-term challenges of global economic instability. Armstrong highlights the importance of understanding market fundamentals amidst a changing world.

Kerry Lutz: Welcome to *The Financial Survival Network*! Spring is around the corner, and in other news, Staten Island Chuck made it through the season without incident—unlike last year. But it doesn't feel like spring in the world economy. Joining us today is Martin

Armstrong. Martin, great to have you back. I hear there's big news about *The Forecaster*. What's happening?

Martin Armstrong: Thanks for having me, Kerry. Yes, there's been some exciting developments. After initially struggling to get a U.S. distributor, we now have one. They stepped up unexpectedly and want to release the film here in just a few weeks. It's already been shown across Europe, Asia, Canada, and even Russia. The U.S. was the only major market where it wasn't planned to air—until now.

Kerry Lutz: Why the delay in the U.S.?

Martin Armstrong: It comes down to self-censorship. When I met with someone from Hollywood, they admitted that discussing topics like government corruption and banks can make it tough to raise funding. This isn't a conspiracy theory; it's a reality in our media landscape. Mainstream outlets cater to corporate and government interests.

Kerry Lutz: That sounds similar to what we've seen with Operation Choke Point. Even trying to access content like your film could be restricted.

Martin Armstrong: Exactly. That's why I started with European distributors. I've experienced media suppression firsthand. For example, Gretchen Morgenson of The New York Times planned a feature on me, but she was suddenly barred from writing about it. The same thing happened at Bloomberg. People think we have a free press, but much of it is controlled by corporate and government interests.

Kerry Lutz: And that's why Edward Snowden had to go to *The Guardian* in the UK.

Martin Armstrong: Right. Every journalist in Washington, D.C., knew about the NSA's surveillance, yet no one reported it. Snowden wouldn't have stood a chance if he'd gone to an American outlet. They'd have handed him over to authorities.

Kerry Lutz: Speaking of surveillance, I remember you've had your own run-ins with government agencies.

Martin Armstrong: Oh, absolutely. After our model predicted Russia's collapse in 1998, the CIA contacted me. They wanted access to our model, even asking me to build something for them. When I declined, things got messy. We experienced sophisticated hacking attempts, and eventually, we traced them back to Langley.

Kerry Lutz: That's unsettling. And now we're seeing China retaliate by demanding backdoor access to technology sold there.

Martin Armstrong: Privacy is dead. Governments worldwide are collecting everything—emails, texts, calls—and storing it indefinitely. The irony is that they collect so much data, they miss actual threats like the Boston bombers.

Kerry Lutz: Let's shift back to the film. When and where can people watch it in the U.S.?

Martin Armstrong: It'll premiere in Los Angeles on March 27th, running three showings daily for a week. After that, it moves to New York in early April with the same schedule. Details are on our site.

Kerry Lutz: Your story is incredible, and the injustice you've faced needs to be heard. But let's talk about the economy. The euro is struggling, and global markets are shaky. What's your outlook for the U.S. stock market?

Martin Armstrong: The U.S. market isn't ready for a major peak yet. I expect it to tread water for now, with a potential rally starting in late 2015 and continuing into 2017. The real driver will be a shift in how people perceive the economy and markets.

Kerry Lutz: Can you elaborate?

Martin Armstrong: Historically, bull markets align with rising interest rates because they reflect economic growth. But since the New Deal, we've been fed propaganda that rising rates are bad. The reality is, markets thrive on anticipation. Lower rates often signal economic trouble.

Kerry Lutz: What about the euro?

Martin Armstrong: The euro is a disaster. It's hitting 12-year lows, and I expect it to eventually break below $0.80. Europe's banking system is heavily tied to government bonds, which are classified as "risk-free." If those bonds devalue significantly, it could wipe out the entire banking system.

Kerry Lutz: And the U.S. dollar?

Martin Armstrong: The dollar will continue to strengthen as it becomes the global safe haven. There's talk of alternatives like the Chinese and Russian systems, but they lack the scale and trust to replace the dollar.

Kerry Lutz: Gold prices have also been volatile. What's happening there?

Martin Armstrong: Gold's decline is tied to the dollar's rise. It's not manipulation; it's market fundamentals. I expect gold to break below $1,000 before stabilizing. Its time will come, but it's not now.

Kerry Lutz: Beyond markets, you've criticized modern education systems. What's your take on apprenticeships?

Martin Armstrong: Apprenticeships are far more effective than traditional schooling for most professions. In places like Switzerland, only 10% of students go to college. The rest learn through hands-on experience, which better prepares them for their careers.

Kerry Lutz: It's a system we could benefit from here. Martin, thanks for your insights and updates on The Forecaster. Best of luck with the film's U.S. release, and we'll catch up soon.

Martin Armstrong: Thanks, Kerry. Always a pleasure.

Key Takeaways:

1. **Censorship in Media:** Armstrong highlights the challenges of distributing The Forecaster in the U.S. due to corporate and government pressures.
2. **Surveillance Concerns:** Governments worldwide are eroding privacy with extensive data collection that often misses critical threats.
3. **Euro's Struggles:** The euro's systemic flaws and ties to devaluing government bonds make it a failing currency.
4. **Gold and Dollar Dynamics:** Gold's decline is tied to the strengthening dollar, driven by market fundamentals.
5. **Education Reform:** Armstrong advocates for apprenticeship models as a more effective alternative to traditional education systems.

Final Thought:

The Forecaster sheds light on systemic issues in global economics and governance, while Armstrong's insights emphasize the need to understand market fundamentals and prepare for an evolving financial landscape.

THE GLOBAL ECONOMIC RECKONING (JULY 15, 2015)

Interview Summary:

In this candid discussion, Martin Armstrong offers a sobering analysis of the global economy, highlighting systemic failures in socialism, the dangers of central banking policies, and the consequences of unchecked government overreach. With his characteristic clarity, Armstrong explains the interconnected forces shaping the financial landscape and warns of the growing strain on global markets, particularly in Europe and the United States.

Armstrong attributes much of the current economic stagnation to rising taxes, government overreach, and the decline in net disposable income. He explains that increasing costs driven by taxes—rather than demand—have created a form of stagflation in which prices rise but economic growth and employment falter. This unsustainable system, he argues, represents the collapse of socialism as governments prioritize self-preservation over reform.

Focusing on Europe, Armstrong critiques the austerity measures imposed on nations like Greece, describing them as a way to protect bondholders at the expense of the populace. He foresees the eventual collapse of the euro system, which he believes is exacerbated by unsustainable debt and economic mismanagement across member states. Similarly, in the U.S., Armstrong warns of a real estate market crash tied to the potential elimination of 30-year mortgages and the broader implications of the government's role in artificially inflating home prices.

He critiques the repeal of the Glass-Steagall Act, transactional banking practices, and banks' increasing dependency on speculative trading rather than lending. Armstrong also laments the erosion of personal freedoms through rising taxes, regulatory overreach, and surveillance, which he believes are symptomatic of a failing system.

On a political note, Armstrong discusses the rise of Donald Trump, framing him as a populist outsider who taps into growing public disillusionment with traditional politics. He also expresses frustration with the media's inability to grasp the broader sentiment driving Trump's appeal.

The conversation concludes with a discussion about *The Forecaster*, the documentary film chronicling Armstrong's life and his controversial forecasts. The film's reception outside the U.S. highlights a growing awareness of corruption in the financial system and a demand for accountability.

Kerry Lutz: What's going on with the world economy? You need to pay attention because so many prognostications miss the mark. But the person you're about to hear from? His forecasts are on a whole other level. You know who I'm talking about—Martin Armstrong. Martin, welcome back! What's happening in the world, and where is the economy heading?

Martin Armstrong: Unfortunately, nowhere but down. We're witnessing the collapse of socialism. People think socialism is about helping others, but in reality, it's about governments helping themselves to your money. They never take responsibility for their failures. Look at Hillary Clinton's economic plan—it's all about forcing companies to increase wages, but there's no discussion of government taking less in taxes.

Kerry Lutz: And this collapse—how does it manifest?

Martin Armstrong: It's creating stagflation. Prices are rising because businesses are passing on their costs, but disposable income is declining due to higher taxes. Small businesses are struggling, hiring less, and unemployment is rising. In New Jersey, for example, office buildings everywhere have "For Rent" signs. Europe is ten times worse, and the deflationary pressures there are immense.

Kerry Lutz: Speaking of Europe—what about Greece? What's going to happen there?

Martin Armstrong: Greece is just the tip of the iceberg. Spain, Portugal, Italy, and even France are in dire straits. Austerity measures are about preserving confidence in bond markets and protecting bankers at the expense of the people. The euro system itself is unsustainable and will eventually collapse.

Kerry Lutz: Central banks seem to be a big part of this problem. What's their role?

Martin Armstrong: Central banks enable governments to inflate bubbles and manipulate markets. But even before central banks, we had financial bubbles—look at the late 1890s when panics occurred almost every two years. The difference now is that banks are trading rather than lending. They've become transactional rather than supporting the economy through business loans.

Kerry Lutz: So, the repeal of Glass-Steagall plays a role here?

Martin Armstrong: Absolutely. The repeal of Glass-Steagall allowed banks to speculate with depositor money. When they make profits, they keep them. When they lose, they demand bailouts, holding governments hostage. This system is fundamentally flawed, and it's why banks constantly need to be rescued.

Kerry Lutz: What about Fannie Mae and Freddie Mac? Should they be eliminated?

Martin Armstrong: If you eliminate them, you also eliminate 30-year mortgages because no one will issue them. That would crash real estate prices. Homes in the $500,000–$600,000 range could drop to $250,000. The government artificially inflated real estate values through these programs, and removing them would create chaos.

Kerry Lutz: It seems like the entire system is designed to benefit banks.

Martin Armstrong: That's correct. Banks profit from fees, and with transactional banking, they offload risk onto others. Mortgages are bundled and sold, leaving no one accountable. During the foreclosure crisis, banks couldn't even prove ownership of loans because they'd been sliced and diced so many times.

Kerry Lutz: So, where does this all lead?

Martin Armstrong: Unfortunately, it leads to collapse. Governments refuse to reform and instead pile on more taxes and regulations. Look at Chicago—property taxes are set to rise 30%. People are being taxed out of their homes, and the government treats taxpayers like an endless source of revenue.

Kerry Lutz: Is privatization the solution?

Martin Armstrong: Yes, absolutely. If pension systems and other programs were privatized, those responsible for mismanagement would face legal consequences. But as it stands, government exempts itself from accountability.

Kerry Lutz: What about Trump? You've written about his rise.

Martin Armstrong: Trump is tapping into a third-party sentiment within the Republican Party. People are fed up with politicians who are bought and controlled. They see Trump as someone who speaks his mind because he isn't beholden to donors. His appeal lies in his ability to say what others won't.

Kerry Lutz: The media doesn't seem to understand his appeal.

Martin Armstrong: Exactly. They think airing his "crazy" statements will hurt him, but it's having the opposite effect. People are tired of traditional politicians, and Trump's defiance resonates.

Kerry Lutz: What about *The Forecaster*? When will we see it in the U.S.?

Martin Armstrong: The film has been well-received in Europe and Canada but hasn't been released in the U.S. or Switzerland—two places where banks are heavily involved. It might end up on Netflix. The goal is to educate people about the corruption in the financial system.

Kerry Lutz: Thanks for your insights, Martin. Everyone, visit ArmstrongEconomics.com to read Martin's latest articles. As always, we'll link to his site from FinancialSurvivalNetwork.com.

Martin Armstrong: Thanks, Kerry. It's always a pleasure.

Key Takeaways:

1. **The Collapse of Socialism:** Governments are failing to deliver on promises, raising taxes, and eroding disposable income, which Armstrong sees as the beginning of socialism's collapse.
2. **The Euro's Fragility:** Greece's troubles are a precursor to broader issues in the eurozone, where austerity measures are protecting bondholders at the expense of citizens.
3. **Real Estate Risks:** The potential elimination of 30-year mortgages could trigger a real estate crash, exposing the fragility of government-inflated markets.
4. **Transactional Banking's Dangers:** Modern banking practices prioritize short-term gains over long-term stability, exacerbating economic fragility.
5. **Trump's Rise:** Trump represents a populist revolt against traditional, donor-controlled politicians, tapping into widespread dissatisfaction with the political system.

6. **The Forecaster's Impact:** The documentary has sparked discussions about financial corruption globally, with hopes of raising awareness in the U.S.

Final Thought:

This interview underscores Armstrong's unique perspective on systemic issues and his ability to anticipate economic and political shifts with remarkable clarity.

THE LOOMING COLLAPSE OF CAREER POLITICS AND GLOBAL ECONOMIES (JANUARY 27, 2016)

Interview Summary:

Kerry Lutz interviews Martin Armstrong, who shares his perspectives on the growing instability in global politics and economics. Armstrong identifies career politicians as the root cause of dysfunction, citing their inability to admit mistakes or implement meaningful reforms. He discusses global discontent, including Europe's refugee crisis, China's economic recalibration, and rising financial constraints in the U.S.

Armstrong critiques government mismanagement, noting how systems like Social Security and Medicare are heading toward insolvency. He highlights the adverse effects of policies like student loans and excessive taxation, arguing that politicians prioritize short-term gains over long-term solutions. He also discusses the stock market, suggesting that global uncertainty will drive money into the private sector, including equities, despite broader economic challenges.

The conversation delves into global real estate trends, with governments like Australia and the U.K. targeting foreign property ownership, pushing investors to places like Florida and New York. Armstrong emphasizes the dangers of debt-servitude policies, such as the U.S. passport revocation law for tax debts, and concludes that only systemic political reform—starting with the removal of career politicians—can address these challenges.

Kerry Lutz: Welcome to *The Financial Survival Network*. I'm Kerry Lutz, and today is January 27, 2016. There's turmoil everywhere, with few solutions in sight. Joining us is Martin Armstrong, whose forecasts have been remarkably accurate. Martin, great to have you back.

Martin Armstrong: Thanks for inviting me.

Kerry Lutz: Things seem to be going from bad to worse globally. What do you see?

Martin Armstrong: The core issue is career politicians. This is why figures like Trump are polling well. People are rejecting the establishment everywhere, not just in the U.S. In Europe, career politicians cling to the euro because their jobs depend on it. If the euro fails, so does Brussels. It's less about society's needs and more about preserving government structures.

In the U.S., 2017 will be critical. Social Security and Medicare go negative, but neither party will act. Republicans don't want the blame for cuts, and Democrats won't address it either. So, nothing happens. Politicians focus on short-term optics rather than real issues.

Kerry Lutz: That's why Trump faces such opposition from the establishment.

Martin Armstrong: Exactly. They only support career politicians who keep the system going. Across Europe, voters are also rejecting the establishment. Scotland removed every Labour Party career politician from Parliament. Catalonia is pushing to leave Spain. People are fed up. As Einstein said, you can't solve problems with the same thinking that created them.

Kerry Lutz: How do we shift to this higher level of thinking?

Martin Armstrong: Historically, it often takes a revolution. I'm not saying Trump is perfect, but he might disrupt the status quo and start necessary debates. Even Bernie Sanders is exposing truths about the Clintons and their Wall Street ties.

For example, the Clintons dismantled Glass-Steagall and pushed for interstate banking, which benefited Wall Street at the expense of average citizens. Their policies turned student loans into non-dischargeable debt, trapping students in lifelong financial servitude.

Kerry Lutz: That bankruptcy law was framed as targeting fraudsters but mainly protected banks from student loan defaults.

Martin Armstrong: Exactly. It echoes Rome's collapse when senators—acting as bankers—enslaved debtors' children to recoup unpaid loans. Today's equivalent is student loans that can't be discharged, leaving graduates in modern-day financial slavery.

Kerry Lutz: And globally, we see more dysfunction. What's your take on China and Russia?

Martin Armstrong: China's growth phase is over. They're now focusing on domestic development, which is smart. Misinterpretation of trade data led many to think China was doing better than it was. Much of the "inflows" were companies borrowing dollars in Hong Kong and reinvesting in China for higher returns—not actual trade growth.

Russia is also struggling, but Europe is the real disaster. Merkel's refugee policies are causing chaos. Germany took in 1.1 million refugees, yet 600,000 are unaccounted for. Borders are closing, and politicians admit that if borders shut, the euro collapses.

Kerry Lutz: Europe's leadership seems disconnected from reality.

Martin Armstrong: Completely. Europe's governing triarchy—the IMF head, ECB president, and EU leader—are all unelected. Citizens can't vote them out, and policies like austerity have deepened the divide.

Kerry Lutz: Turning back to the U.S., what about proposals to replace the Federal Reserve or implement public banking?

Martin Armstrong: Those ideas don't address the root problem: government incompetence. It's not about who creates money but how it's managed. In December, the government quietly created a trillion dollars without anyone noticing. They also added a law allowing the IRS to revoke passports for $50,000 in unpaid taxes or penalties. That's modern debt servitude.

Kerry Lutz: History repeating itself, as always.

Martin Armstrong: Absolutely. The Roman Empire required tax payment proof for travel—essentially the first passports. Today, we're heading down the same path.

Kerry Lutz: Can someone like Trump fix this, or is the system too entrenched?

Martin Armstrong: One person can't overhaul the system, but Trump could at least start debates and resist rubber-stamping bad policies. His appeal lies in his independence from Wall Street. Compare that to Cruz or the Clintons, who have deep ties to Goldman Sachs.

Kerry Lutz: Let's talk markets. What's your outlook for the Dow?

Martin Armstrong: Our models suggest the market will extend its growth cycle until 2020. As trust in government erodes, capital will flow into the private sector. People park money where they perceive safety, even if it means accepting lower returns.

Kerry Lutz: What about real estate?

Martin Armstrong: Real estate varies. In the U.S., Florida and New York are benefiting from international capital fleeing restrictive policies in places like Australia and the U.K., which now heavily regulate foreign property ownership. But overall, property markets are under pressure from excessive taxation and regulatory crackdowns.

Kerry Lutz: It's shortsighted governance, isn't it?

Martin Armstrong: Completely. Governments are focused on immediate survival, ignoring long-term consequences. Most officials care little about what happens after their tenure because they're insulated with pensions and perks.

Kerry Lutz: So, the solution?

Martin Armstrong: Remove career politicians. Our system was designed for citizen legislators, not lifelong bureaucrats. But now they've entrenched themselves with salaries, pensions, and unchecked power. Real reform is necessary.

Kerry Lutz: Martin, as always, thanks for your insights. For those listening, check out Martin's work at ArmstrongEconomics.com and subscribe to his updates. Stay informed, and let's hope for positive change.

Martin Armstrong: Thanks, Kerry. It's better to know what's coming and prepare than to be blindsided.

Key Takeaways:

1. **Career Politicians:** Entrenched officials prioritize short-term survival over long-term reform, perpetuating systemic failures.
2. **Global Instability:** Europe faces a refugee crisis and economic struggles, with the euro on the brink of collapse.
3. **Economic Challenges:** U.S. programs like Social Security and Medicare face insolvency, while excessive taxation and regulatory policies stifle growth.
4. **Market Dynamics:** The Dow and real estate markets attract capital as safe havens amidst global uncertainty.
5. **Systemic Reform:** Genuine change requires removing career politicians and addressing governance at its core.

Final Thought:

As global economies teeter on the edge of instability, systemic reform—rooted in accountability and long-term thinking—remains crucial for sustainable progress.

A GLOBAL CONFIDENCE CRISIS: NAVIGATING POLITICAL AND ECONOMIC UPHEAVAL (MARCH 28, 2017)

Interview Summary:

In this dialogue, Martin Armstrong examines the political and economic shifts under the early Trump administration and their implications for global markets. He highlights how confidence in governments and institutions underpins cycles of political unrest, economic instability, and financial markets. Armstrong also discusses the broader global phenomenon of rising dissatisfaction with traditional political systems and the eventual transition of financial power from the West to China.

Kerry Lutz: Welcome back to *The Financial Survival Network*. Today is March 28th, 2017. The first quarter of the year is almost done, and Trump has been in office for just over 70 days. Let's check in with Martin Armstrong to see where we're headed. Martin, always a pleasure to have you on.

Martin Armstrong: Thank you for inviting me.

Kerry Lutz: So, Trump's in office now, and the fallout has been remarkable. Many are unhappy with the election outcome and seem determined to block him at every turn. Where do we go from here?

Martin Armstrong: Well, our computer correctly forecasted his win, though I wasn't sure if the election would be manipulated. Trump won decisively in the Electoral College, and if you exclude California—a questionable outlier—he even dominated the popular vote. The left, however, is fighting tooth and nail to prevent reforms. This talk about Russia interfering in the election is mostly noise. Even if we assume Putin released the DNC emails, no one has claimed that the information itself was false. What they're upset about is getting caught, not that the election process was genuinely compromised.

Kerry Lutz: It seems the media is amplifying this discord.

Martin Armstrong: Absolutely. The U.S. press today operates more like Pravda during the Soviet era, preaching the party line rather than reporting the truth. Even honest journalists have their stories rewritten by editors to fit a narrative. Mainstream media are major corporations with vested interests, no different from Wall Street firms. This isn't about journalism; it's about paybacks and influence. What we're seeing is a revolution—not just in the U.S., but globally. Governments everywhere have borrowed recklessly since World War II with no intention of repaying their debts, and now standards of living are declining. People are reaching a breaking point.

Kerry Lutz: Let's talk about Obamacare. What's your take on its economic impact?

Martin Armstrong: Obamacare is effectively a tax disguised as healthcare reform. The Supreme Court upheld it because it viewed the mandate as a tax. Instead of addressing uninsured individuals directly, Obamacare forced younger people to buy insurance they didn't need or face penalties. I experienced this firsthand—my premiums doubled. My initial policy was canceled because it didn't include maternity leave. When I explained I didn't need that coverage, they said it didn't matter. The law required it. This burden disproportionately affects the younger generation, who are already saddled with student debt and a lack of job opportunities.

Kerry Lutz: It sounds like a setup for generational conflict.

Martin Armstrong: Exactly. In the U.S., the average age of kids still living with their parents has risen into their 30s. Europe has an even graver issue—youth unemployment is over 60% in some areas. This is dangerous because high youth unemployment historically leads to revolutions. What governments don't realize is that their policies are creating the conditions for social unrest. Obamacare, student loan policies, and stagnant wages are crushing the younger generation.

Kerry Lutz: Trump has been a lightning rod for both sides of the political spectrum. What's driving this unprecedented backlash?

Martin Armstrong: Trump represents a third-party movement, even though he ran as a Republican. His own party opposed him at every turn. This political divide is reflective of broader societal unrest. Historically, civil wars and revolutions arise from class struggles, not racial or religious differences. We've reached a point where the gap between the rich and poor is being exploited politically. The media and political elites are playing with fire by fueling these divisions. Historically, this is how revolutions and collapses begin.

Kerry Lutz: What does the future hold for the U.S.?

Martin Armstrong: Our computer models predict that the financial capital of the world will shift from the U.S. to China by 2032, much like how it moved from Britain to the U.S. in 1914. This doesn't mean the U.S. will collapse, but it will lose its dominant position. Western society is in decline, partly due to corruption and unsustainable policies. The post-World War II era of unlimited borrowing and spending is coming to an end.

Kerry Lutz: Let's pivot to the markets. Where are we headed with stocks, precious metals, and Bitcoin?

Martin Armstrong: The stock market is consolidating, but it's still on track to double from here. Most analysts fail because they look at markets through a domestic lens. You have to understand global capital flows. For example, Eurostat recently reported a net capital outflow from Europe in 2016 for the first time. Foreign investors sold $192 billion in Eurobonds last year, compared to $30 billion in purchases the year before. That money went into equities—not gold—because institutions need a place to park large sums of money.

Kerry Lutz: Why isn't gold benefiting from this?

Martin Armstrong: Gold thrives during crises of confidence in government. It's not about inflation or fiat currency, despite what some promoters claim. The last major gold high in 1980, adjusted for inflation, is $2,300. We haven't broken that yet. Gold will rise, but not until after 2018 when confidence in governments erodes further. People need to stop focusing on inflation and start looking at trust in institutions.

Kerry Lutz: What about Bitcoin and electronic currency?

Martin Armstrong: Bitcoin has been a tool for people in places like China to move money out of the country. That's why the Chinese government is cracking down on it. Governments want to eliminate cash and move toward electronic money to increase tax compliance and prevent bank runs. The shift to electronic currency will make gold more relevant as a way to stay "off the grid."

Kerry Lutz: You've long predicted trouble for the euro. Where do we stand now?

Martin Armstrong: The euro is structurally flawed. Without federal bonds, every bank relies on state-level bonds for reserves. If Greece defaults, banks holding Greek bonds are in trouble. The ECB has only made things worse by introducing negative interest rates. Our models project that the euro could collapse entirely by 2020. The upcoming French elections are pivotal—if Le Pen wins, the euro could unravel quickly. Even if she loses, Brussels will take it as a validation of their policies and double down, delaying the inevitable collapse.

Kerry Lutz: It sounds dire. Is there any hope for reform?

Martin Armstrong: Not without significant pain first. Governments don't reform unless they're forced to by crisis. Europe's banking system is far more vulnerable than the U.S.'s. If capital flight continues, the ECB won't be able to stabilize the system.

Kerry Lutz: Martin, any closing thoughts?

Martin Armstrong: The global crisis we're seeing isn't just political or economic—it's a crisis of confidence. When people stop trusting governments and institutions, you see shifts in markets, revolutions, and systemic resets. Precious metals will rise when that confidence collapses, but we're not quite there yet. Until then, watch for signs in political elections and capital flows. These are the real indicators of what's to come.

Kerry Lutz: Always a pleasure, Martin. Where can listeners find your work?

Martin Armstrong: Visit ArmstrongEconomics.com. We have upcoming World Economic Conferences in Hong Kong and Orlando later this year.

Kerry Lutz: Thanks, Martin. We'll talk again soon.

Martin Armstrong: Thank you, and good luck to everyone.

Key Takeaways:

1. **Political Division:** Trump's presidency highlights the rise of third-party movements and the growing dissatisfaction with traditional political systems.
2. **Global Economic Shift:** The financial capital of the world is projected to move from the U.S. to China by 2032.

3. **Market Trends:** The stock market remains strong due to global capital flows, but gold will rise only when confidence in governments erodes significantly.
4. **The Euro's Flaws:** Structural issues make the euro unsustainable, with a potential collapse by 2020.
5. **Electronic Currency:** The move toward cashless economies will drive renewed interest in gold as a way to maintain privacy and independence.

Final Thought:

This chapter encapsulates Armstrong's analysis of a world in flux, offering valuable insights into the interplay between politics, economics, and market behavior.

UNRAVELING GLOBAL AND ECONOMIC TRENDS (SEPTEMBER 27, 2017)

Interview Summary:

In this engaging dialogue, Martin Armstrong illuminates the shifting global political and economic landscape. He addresses the challenges faced by governments, the evolution of the eurozone, the trajectory of the U.S. dollar, and the roles of cryptocurrencies, gold, and stock markets in these dynamics. Armstrong underlines the significance of confidence in governments and markets, linking it to societal and financial stability.

Kerry Lutz: Today is September 27, 2017. It's been an eventful quarter—storms, Bitcoin's volatility, political chaos. To put things in perspective, we have Martin Armstrong of ArmstrongEconomics.com. Martin, welcome back!

Martin Armstrong: Thank you for inviting me.

Kerry Lutz: It's been quite a quarter, Martin. What's your take on where things are heading?

Martin Armstrong: It's been chaotic, to say the least. From Brexit to Trump's election, it's a period I've labeled "the year from political hell." We've just seen the German elections—Merkel lost 9% of the vote. That's not surprising to me, though it seems to have caught many off guard. She's been living in a bubble. And now we have Catalonia, where Madrid is sending troops to suppress the referendum. It's showcasing the authoritarian tendencies still lingering in Spain since Franco's era.

Kerry Lutz: That's a strong statement.

Martin Armstrong: But it's true. Governments rarely change their fundamental behavior, regardless of who is in power. We saw it with Obama—he criticized Guantanamo Bay, the NSA, and unconstitutional practices but expanded those very policies once in office. Greece elected a left-wing government to fight austerity, yet they reinforced it. Real political change requires a revolution, and that's what many societies are inching toward.

Kerry Lutz: Can Trump bridge the partisan divide in the U.S.?

Martin Armstrong: I doubt it. The Democratic Party has been in a bear market since FDR—lower highs and lower lows. It's not just the U.S., though. Socialist parties across Europe are collapsing. In Germany, the SPD got its lowest support ever, at 20%. Why? Because socialism has largely been about raising taxes, which erodes living standards. Even Trump faces opposition within his own party. The political elites in both major U.S. parties don't recognize the silent majority who voted for him. This discontent isn't limited to America. Catalonia's independence movement and Brexit are symptoms of a broader dissatisfaction with centralized governance.

Kerry Lutz: How does all this affect the Eurozone?

Martin Armstrong: The euro is fundamentally flawed. Merkel is its face, and her weakened position after the elections only underscores the currency's fragility. Macron in France wants to federalize Europe and impose new euro-wide taxes, but this is a desperate move to save France's crumbling finances and pension system. The Eurozone's structure is untenable. Member states issue their own bonds, and the banking system is a mess. Banks rely on state bonds as reserves, so a default in one country—like Greece—threatens the entire system. It's unsustainable.

Kerry Lutz: What's your outlook for the U.S. dollar?

114

Martin Armstrong: The dollar will rise in the coming years, but that's not necessarily good for the U.S. economy. A stronger dollar worsens the trade deficit and hurts exports. Historically, the U.S. has always sought to weaken the dollar to stay competitive. For example, Roosevelt devalued the dollar in 1934, and the G5 agreement in 1985 was designed to bring it down. But Europe's instability is driving capital into the U.S. Banks in Europe are even parking money in the Federal Reserve to avoid negative rates. It's a dire situation for the Eurozone.

Kerry Lutz: Cryptocurrency has been making waves. What's your take?

Martin Armstrong: Cryptocurrencies like Bitcoin are speculative assets. Governments won't tolerate competition in currency. The U.S. is already requiring travelers to declare more than $10,000 in electronic currency, and it won't stop there. Eventually, we'll see government-controlled digital currencies. As for gold, it's still not ready to break out. Gold rises when confidence in governments collapses. It's not about inflation or fiat currency fears—it's about a lack of trust.

Kerry Lutz: So what's holding gold back?

Martin Armstrong: Reporting requirements and restrictions make gold less liquid than it used to be. The system needs to crack first—like in 1934 or 1985—before gold can rally significantly.

Kerry Lutz: What about the stock market? Is it still the best place to park money?

Martin Armstrong: Absolutely. There's nowhere else for large capital to go. Institutional investors are shifting from government bonds to equities. Norway's sovereign wealth fund, the largest in the world, moved from bonds to stocks in 2013 and is now the only solvent pension fund globally. Governments' mounting debt and pension liabilities are pushing institutions toward private assets. Stocks are benefiting from this capital shift, and the market still has room to double before this cycle ends.

Kerry Lutz: What's the key takeaway from all this?

Martin Armstrong: Confidence is everything. The global political and economic system is in flux, and institutions are scrambling to adapt. Whether it's the euro, the dollar, or gold, the underlying driver is confidence in governments and markets.

Kerry Lutz: Thank you, Martin, for your insights. Where can listeners find more of your work?

Martin Armstrong: Visit ArmstrongEconomics.com. There's plenty of analysis and resources there.

Kerry Lutz: Thanks for joining us, Martin. Talk again soon.

Martin Armstrong: Always a pleasure. Take care.

Key Takeaways:

1. **Political Fractures**: Global dissatisfaction with governance is driving movements like Brexit and Catalonia's independence push.
2. **Eurozone Weakness**: Structural flaws in the Eurozone make it increasingly unstable.
3. **Rising Dollar**: A strong dollar benefits capital flows but exacerbates trade deficits.
4. **Cryptocurrency Risks**: Governments are unlikely to allow private digital currencies to flourish unchecked.
5. **Gold's Future**: Gold will rally when systemic cracks deepen and confidence erodes.
6. **Stock Market Strength**: Equities remain the preferred asset class for large institutional capital.

Final Thought:

This chapter captures the evolving dynamics of global markets and the underlying forces shaping them, offering insights for navigating uncertain times.

ECONOMIC SHIFTS AND GLOBAL REACTIONS (DECEMBER 27, 2017)

Interview Summary:

In this wide-ranging discussion, Martin Armstrong dissects the sweeping implications of the 2017 U.S. tax reform, its impact on global markets, and the broader economic and political dynamics at play. From corporate competitiveness to the shifting tides of international capital, Armstrong provides insights into how these changes are influencing America's economy, stock markets, and the world at large.

Kerry Lutz: Welcome to *The Financial Survival Network*. It's December 27, 2017—just four days left in the year! Big news: the tax bill has passed. We've got shifts in the economy and international ripple effects. Who better to discuss this than Martin Armstrong, whose predictions are uncannily accurate? Martin, welcome back, and Happy New Year!

Martin Armstrong: Thanks for having me.

Kerry Lutz: The tax bill is causing waves. What's your take?

Martin Armstrong: It's monumental. The American press hasn't grasped the international panic it's sparked. Germany, the UK, and even China are alarmed. I just had emergency meetings in Brussels and London—everyone's scrambling. U.S. corporations are taxed on worldwide income, which, until now, made them uncompetitive globally.

For years, I've argued that our corporate tax rates needed to be slashed to at least 15%, like Hong Kong. Back in 1996, I testified before

Congress, explaining why U.S. firms couldn't compete abroad. Foreign companies don't face the same tax burdens, and now, with this reform, American businesses have a fighting chance.

Kerry Lutz: Critics claim this will only benefit big corporations. What's your response?

Martin Armstrong: That's a shortsighted argument. While some large firms may use repatriated cash for stock buybacks, the money doesn't vanish. Pension funds, which hold much of these stocks, will reinvest in other companies, creating more opportunities.

The real game-changer is for small businesses. They're the backbone of job creation, and this reform directly benefits them. For larger corporations, it's better to repatriate profits and face a reduced tax rate than leave the money offshore, where it does nothing for the U.S. economy.

Kerry Lutz: Eliminating state and local tax deductions is controversial. What's your take?

Martin Armstrong: It's long overdue. High-tax states like California and New York have relied on federal subsidies for years. Removing these deductions forces people to pay closer attention to local politics and accountability.

Take New Jersey, for example. When they introduced income taxes, they sold it as "free money" because you'd get a federal deduction. Now, those states are facing an exodus. People and businesses are moving to low-tax states like Texas and Florida, which are already seeing booming real estate markets.

Kerry Lutz: How is the world reacting to these changes?

Martin Armstrong: The tax reform has sparked fear abroad. Countries like China and Germany worry they can't compete with a revitalized America. Europe, in particular, is a mess. Merkel is weakened, and there's growing unrest in Italy, Catalonia, and elsewhere. Calls for a "United States of Europe" are gaining traction, but cultural and linguistic divisions make that vision impossible.

Kerry Lutz: Will this reform be an economic shot in the arm?

Martin Armstrong: Absolutely. Growth is likely to hit 4% in 2018, which will be a major win for Trump. The stock market will continue its upward trajectory as capital flows into the U.S. from struggling economies abroad.

However, Europe's issues, from failing pension systems to overregulation, will keep their economies stagnant. Countries like Italy and Spain are already experiencing capital flight, and the U.S. remains the only safe haven.

Kerry Lutz: What about gold and the dollar?

Martin Armstrong: Gold isn't ready for a breakout just yet. For gold to surge, there needs to be a collapse in confidence—likely triggered by instability in Europe or Japan. As for the dollar, it will strengthen further as capital continues flowing into the U.S.

The stock market, meanwhile, is poised to soar. Once it breaks 25,000, resistance will be at 28,000, and after that, we're looking at 36,000. It's a hated bull market, much like the one in the 1920s. The shortage of stocks due to buybacks and limited IPOs will only fuel this rally.

Kerry Lutz: You called Trump's election. What's your assessment of his presidency so far?

Martin Armstrong: Trump is a disruptor, and that's exactly what the system needed. He's doing what he promised, which baffles career politicians. His tax reform is the first major structural change since Reagan, and it's shaking the status quo.

The Democrats are doubling down on class warfare and impeachment rhetoric, but they're missing the bigger picture. Their high-tax states are losing ground, and their opposition to Trump's reforms will likely cost them in the midterms.

Kerry Lutz: Final thoughts on where we're headed?

Martin Armstrong: 2018 will bring higher volatility, but the U.S. is positioned for growth. Europe, on the other hand, is teetering. Between political instability, capital flight, and cultural divides, they're in for a tough road ahead.

Kerry Lutz: Thanks for joining us, Martin. As always, your insights are invaluable. Happy New Year!

Martin Armstrong: Thanks, Kerry. Happy New Year to you, too.

Key Takeaways:

1. **U.S. Tax Reform:** A transformative policy that levels the global playing field for American businesses.
2. **State and Local Tax Deductions:** Forces accountability in high-tax states, driving migration to low-tax regions.
3. **Global Reactions:** Europe and Asia are struggling to adapt to a more competitive U.S. economy.
4. **Stock Market Outlook:** The bull market is far from over, with significant upside potential.
5. **Capital Flow:** The U.S. remains a safe haven amidst global instability.
6. **Gold and Dollar:** Gold's breakout hinges on a loss of confidence in governments, while the dollar strengthens due to capital inflows.

Final Thought:

This chapter offers a snapshot of a pivotal moment in economic history, setting the stage for dramatic shifts in global power dynamics and market opportunities.

MARCHING TOWARD CHANGE: GLOBAL SHIFTS (MARCH 12, 2018)

Interview Summary:

Martin Armstrong examines global developments, including North Korea's surprising overtures, Europe's growing instability, and the evolving dynamics of U.S. economic policy. Drawing on historical cycles and real-time geopolitical insights, he outlines the challenges and opportunities facing major powers while casting an eye on looming monetary crises and market volatility.

Kerry Lutz: Welcome to *The Financial Survival Network*. Today is March 12, 2018. With North Korea, Europe, and the economy in flux, what's next? As always, we're joined by Martin Armstrong of *Armstrong Economics* for insights you won't find anywhere else. Martin, welcome back.

Martin Armstrong: Thank you for having me, Kerry.

Kerry Lutz: Let's start with North Korea. Is this thaw in relations genuine, or is there something else going on?

Martin Armstrong: North Korea's shift is more a reflection of desperation than goodwill. Historically, leaders like Kim Jong Un resort to external conflicts to deflect from internal crises. His economy is struggling, and his people are suffering. He knows a war with the U.S. would end disastrously, so talking is his only option.

China plays a key role here. They won't tolerate nuclear conflict in their backyard. While people envision catastrophic scenarios, including nuclear war, the reality is more complex. The environmental and geopolitical blowback from such a conflict would deter all parties involved.

Kerry Lutz: So North Korea isn't the greatest threat. Where is the real danger?

Martin Armstrong: Europe is the bigger tinderbox. Russia's economy is weak, but it's heavily armed and governed by oligarchs. When governments face domestic unrest, they often seek external enemies. Historically, it's a choice between reform or deflection. Russia has chosen deflection, and this could escalate tensions, especially with NATO.

The Middle East is another flashpoint, particularly the rising conflict between Saudi Arabia and Iran. This Sunni-Shiite divide mirrors historical religious wars like those in Northern Europe. As both economies falter, they're likely to intensify their rivalry, dragging global powers like the U.S. and Russia into the fray.

Kerry Lutz: Let's pivot to the U.S. economy. What's driving its resilience?

Martin Armstrong: The U.S. is benefiting from global instability. Capital is flowing into American markets because Europe and other regions are struggling. The U.S. has also become the world's largest oil producer, thanks to fracking. This undermines the influence of traditional oil powers like Saudi Arabia and Russia.

The recent stock market correction wasn't a cause for panic. It's a natural pause after eight years of growth. The first half of 2018 will likely be choppy, but this isn't the crash that the bears have been predicting.

Kerry Lutz: What about pensions? Many states and countries seem to be on the brink.

Martin Armstrong: The pension crisis is massive and global. Most funds require 8% returns to meet liabilities, but they're stuck buying bonds yielding 3% or less. This traditional portfolio mix—60% equities and 40% bonds—is no longer viable.

In Europe, the ECB owns over 40% of government debt, artificially propping up bond markets. If they stop buying, no institution would touch these bonds at current rates. The Fed, in contrast, is unwinding its balance sheet responsibly. Critics often bash the Fed, but compared to Europe, it's handling the situation far better.

Kerry Lutz: What's your outlook for gold and the dollar?

Martin Armstrong: Gold will rise eventually, but not until confidence in governments erodes significantly. Right now, only about 7% of people are concerned about economic instability. That number needs to hit 25–30% before we see a major move in gold.

As for the dollar, it remains the world's reserve currency, and there's no real competition. The euro is fragile, and other currencies lack global trust. The dollar's strength may hurt gold in the short term, but it's also what makes U.S. markets a safe haven.

Kerry Lutz: What lies ahead for the markets and the economy?

Martin Armstrong: The stock market will continue to climb, confounding critics. We're in a long-term bull market driven by international capital flows. While 2018 will see consolidation, the real fireworks will start after July.

Looking further ahead, 2021 will be pivotal. It's the year after the next U.S. presidential election and marks the start of a monetary crisis cycle. This could lead to reforms similar to Bretton Woods, though full resolution might not come until 2032.

Kerry Lutz: As always, your insights are invaluable, Martin. Final thoughts?

Martin Armstrong: We're at the start of a transformative period. Expect volatility but also opportunities. The U.S. remains the anchor in an unstable world, but the real challenges will emerge globally in the coming years.

Kerry Lutz: Thank you, Martin.

Key Takeaways:

1. **North Korea**: Talks are a survival strategy, not a peace breakthrough.
2. **Europe and Russia**: Europe's instability and Russia's deflection tactics pose greater risks than North Korea.
3. **Middle East**: The Saudi-Iran rivalry is a dangerous flashpoint with global implications.
4. **U.S. Markets**: Capital inflows and energy independence are driving growth, despite market corrections.
5. **Pensions**: The global pension crisis is worsening, with no easy solutions.
6. **Future Cycles**: The next major monetary crisis is looming, with 2021 as a critical turning point.

Final Thought:

This chapter captures a moment of economic and geopolitical flux, providing a roadmap for navigating the challenges ahead.

POLITICAL UPHEAVAL AND GLOBAL FINANCIAL STRAINS (JULY 23, 2018)

Interview Summary:

Martin Armstrong examines the systemic governance issues plaguing nations globally, from Italy's struggles within the EU to America's political landscape under Trump. Armstrong delves into the rise of revolutionary sentiments, economic mismanagement, and the increasing tension between governments and citizens. With topics spanning Bitcoin, gold, constitutional principles, and geopolitical strategies, this chapter highlights the growing demand for accountability and structural reform.

Kerry Lutz: Does anyone think long-term anymore? Governments seem to be living for today with no concern for future generations. To explore these challenges, we're joined by Martin Armstrong from ArmstrongEconomics.com. Martin, welcome back!

Martin Armstrong: Thanks for inviting me.

Kerry Lutz: You've mentioned Italy could face a revolution soon. Can you elaborate?

Martin Armstrong: Italy is a prime example of economic mismanagement. Real estate has historically been the primary form of savings for Italians, but EU-imposed taxes are eroding this stability. The introduction of high sales and inheritance taxes has created a one-way market where everyone wants to sell, but no one can buy.

Brussels and the IMF continue pushing for tax hikes, ignoring the long-term consequences. This mirrors the S&L crisis in the U.S., where policy changes led to a market collapse. If Italy doesn't address these issues, a revolution could erupt by 2021.

Kerry Lutz: Why do governments seem incapable of planning ahead?

Martin Armstrong: It's a systemic failure. Politicians prioritize short-term gains over long-term stability. For instance, New Jersey's water tax—disguised as a "fee"—is just another way to extract money from citizens. Such measures reflect a lack of financial management skills.

Globally, this issue isn't limited to Italy. The "Trump revolution" highlights a growing discontent with traditional governance, where people are voting out entrenched politicians. It's not about left or right; it's about rejecting the status quo.

Kerry Lutz: How do you view Trump's presidency in this context?

Martin Armstrong: Trump is a disruptor, and that's why he faces such resistance. He challenges the deep-seated bureaucracy, or "deep state," which fights back at every turn. From trade negotiations to addressing NATO contributions, Trump's actions are forcing systemic change.

However, the opposition is relentless. Even meetings like the one with Putin are sabotaged by internal forces, such as the Justice Department's ill-timed indictments.

Kerry Lutz: Europe seems to be teetering. What's your outlook for the Eurozone?

Martin Armstrong: The Euro is on borrowed time. Countries like Italy, already struggling under EU mandates, are rebelling. Merkel's unilateral refugee policy further exacerbated tensions, forcing nations like Italy to take on burdens they can't afford.

Capital flight is accelerating, and the Euro's value continues to decline. At its core, the EU prioritizes preserving its structure over addressing its people's needs. This authoritarian approach will lead to the Euro's eventual collapse.

Kerry Lutz: What's the future for Bitcoin and gold?

Martin Armstrong: Bitcoin's heyday is over. Governments won't allow a decentralized currency to undermine their control. Most countries are cracking down on cryptocurrency use, particularly for money laundering.

Gold, on the other hand, rises when confidence in governments collapses. While not ready for a breakout yet, it will shine when systemic instability becomes unavoidable. However, modern regulations make gold less practical than before.

Kerry Lutz: You've been critical of the justice system. What's the core issue?

Martin Armstrong: The U.S. justice system is fundamentally unfair. Laws can be passed without initial scrutiny, placing the burden on citizens to challenge them. Judicial deference to the executive branch has inverted constitutional principles, turning restraints on government into tools of control over the people.

Globally, this systemic failure fuels revolutions. Governments push until people push back. Historically, revolutions arise not because people suddenly wake up, but because unsustainable systems finally collapse.

Kerry Lutz: What's your forecast for the near future?

Martin Armstrong: Expect greater volatility. The U.S. remains relatively stable, but Europe is nearing a breaking point. By 2021, global financial systems could face a significant reset. Whether it's through revolution or reform, systemic change is inevitable.

Kerry Lutz: Always a pleasure, Martin. Thanks for your insights.

Martin Armstrong: Thank you, Kerry.

Key Takeaways:

1. **Italy's Crisis**: EU tax policies are destabilizing Italy, possibly leading to revolution by 2021.
2. **Governance Issues**: Short-term thinking and poor management plague governments globally.
3. **Trump's Impact**: Despite fierce resistance, Trump's policies are reshaping global politics.
4. **Eurozone Instability**: Capital flight and authoritarian policies are accelerating the Euro's decline.
5. **Cryptocurrency and Gold**: Cryptos face regulatory crackdowns, while gold awaits a collapse in government confidence.
6. **Systemic Failure**: Governance and justice systems worldwide are driving revolutionary sentiments.

Final Thought:

This chapter captures the growing discontent with traditional governance and the systemic flaws that threaten global stability. The world is on the brink of transformative changes, with political and financial upheavals looming.

ECONOMIC CHALLENGES, CRYPTOCURRENCIES, AND PENSIONS (JANUARY 15, 2019)

Interview Summary:

Martin Armstrong delves into the interconnected issues of gold, cryptocurrencies, and the global pension crisis. He explores the implications of declining confidence in governments, the economic risks posed by emerging markets, and the role of the Federal Reserve. With insights into geopolitical strategies and personal anecdotes, this chapter underscores the mounting pressures on financial systems and governance.

Kerry Lutz: Gold is rising, and so are other tangible assets. Does this reflect a growing distrust in governments?

Martin Armstrong: Absolutely. When people begin to see government as the problem, they look for alternatives. This isn't limited to savvy investors—eventually, the average person on the street will come to the same realization.

When that shift in perception happens, we'll see a surge in tangible assets like gold, silver, and even the stock market. This reflects a broader collapse in confidence in government-issued currency and bonds. Historically, this pattern played out between 1975 and 1980 when gold hit $875, and the stock market also rose significantly.

Kerry Lutz: What's your forecast for the coming years?

Martin Armstrong: Starting in 2021, we'll likely see an inflationary cycle lasting through 2024. Civil unrest will escalate, particularly as we approach the 2020 presidential elections. These factors will push people to invest more aggressively in tangible assets.

As for the stock market, the current decline has created buying opportunities. Unless the Dow closes below 21,600 on a monthly basis, there's no reason to expect a major crash. Gold's breakout level remains $1,362, but it could dip below $1,000 briefly, triggering bearish sentiment before rebounding strongly.

Kerry Lutz: You've often said markets are driven by emotion. Can you elaborate?

Martin Armstrong: Markets are psychological. At the lows, everyone believes prices will never recover; at the highs, they think the rally will never end. For example, in 2009, I predicted new highs for the stock market, and many dismissed it as a joke.

The same pattern will play out for gold. If it briefly breaks below $1,000, people will call it the end of gold. But that's when the real rally begins, driven by short-sellers who get stopped out repeatedly. This emotional cycle fuels the market's ascent.

Kerry Lutz: What's your take on Bitcoin and cryptocurrencies?

Martin Armstrong: Cryptocurrencies represent an anti-government stance, which is why they face increasing regulation. Governments have studied the technology, and while they appreciate its potential for control—such as eliminating cash—they won't allow private cryptocurrencies to thrive.

Bitcoin, for instance, isn't practical as a medium of exchange. Its limited usability and the small number of global nodes make it vulnerable. Governments can easily impose restrictions, treating it like cash for declaration purposes.

Kerry Lutz: Let's shift to pensions. How serious is this issue?

Martin Armstrong: The pension crisis is catastrophic. Governments and corporations are struggling to fulfill their obligations. For example, many U.S. states like Illinois can't legally modify their pension plans due to court rulings.

This unsustainable system forces employers to hire part-time workers to avoid pension liabilities while older employees face layoffs to reduce costs. Public sector employees often enjoy benefits, such as lifetime healthcare, that private sector workers can't access. These imbalances are bankrupting states and municipalities.

Kerry Lutz: What role does governance play in these systemic issues?

Martin Armstrong: The deep state—the entrenched bureaucracy—has accumulated immense power, beginning with George W. Bush and extending through Obama. This unelected system resists any outsider, such as Trump, who threatens its control.

Trump's presidency highlights the tension between career politicians and reformers. The real challenge lies in what comes after Trump. Career politicians are likely to reassert control, perpetuating the status quo.

Kerry Lutz: Where do we go from here?

Martin Armstrong: Ultimately, we're heading toward significant change, likely after 2032. Until then, the focus will remain on short-term solutions that ignore the larger systemic problems. Without reform, we'll see increasing civil unrest, financial instability, and political turmoil.

Kerry Lutz: Always a pleasure, Martin. Thank you for sharing your insights.

Martin Armstrong: Thank you, Kerry.

Key Takeaways:

1. **Gold and Tangible Assets**: Rising as confidence in government declines, with an inflationary cycle expected from 2021 to 2024.
2. **Cryptocurrency Regulation**: Governments are unlikely to allow private cryptocurrencies to thrive long-term.
3. **Pension Crisis**: Unsustainable systems are forcing layoffs, part-time work, and financial strain on states.
4. **Market Psychology**: Emotional cycles drive markets, creating opportunities amidst bearish sentiment.
5. **Deep State Dynamics**: Entrenched bureaucracies resist reform, threatening long-term stability.

Final Thought:

This chapter underscores the interconnected crises of financial systems, governance, and public confidence, painting a complex picture of global challenges.

GLOBAL ECONOMIC TRENDS, CONFIDENCE IN GOVERNMENT, AND FINANCIAL REALITIES (JUNE 28, 2019)

Interview Summary:

In this episode of *The Financial Survival Network*, host Kerry Lutz engages with Martin Armstrong of Armstrong Economics to discuss global economic shifts, the implications of central bank policies, and the growing mistrust in government. They cover topics ranging from inflation cycles and interest rates to government manipulation, geopolitical instability, and the future of education and small businesses.

Kerry Lutz: Welcome to *The Financial Survival Network*. It's June 28, 2019. Don't forget to join our Bitcoin contest—details are on the website. But for now, we're joined by Martin Armstrong. Martin, great to have you back. Let's jump right into it. Gold seems to be breaking out. What's your take?

Martin Armstrong: Thanks, Kerry. Gold has cleared its first resistance level, which is promising, but this is just part of a summer rally. The real action will align with a broader economic cycle, particularly the next inflationary business cycle, which I expect to peak around 2024.

Right now, we're in a phase where confidence in government is eroding—a key driver for inflation. People don't understand that inflation isn't just about money supply; it's about perception. Back in 1980, during the OPEC crisis, the belief that prices would only rise led to hoarding. That's the psychology driving inflation, not quantitative easing.

Kerry Lutz: What role are central banks playing in this?

Martin Armstrong: Central banks have completely failed. Historically, the Federal Reserve stimulated the economy by buying corporate paper. But during World War I, the government redirected that focus to fund war efforts, and it never returned.

Now, central banks like the ECB are propping up governments by buying massive amounts of government debt. In Europe, the ECB owns 40% of national debts. This keeps governments on life support, but it does nothing for the private sector.

Confidence in central banks is collapsing because their policies haven't worked. Quantitative easing has led to deflation, not inflation, because people don't trust the economy. They're hoarding cash instead of spending or investing.

Kerry Lutz: So when does this confidence collapse trigger inflation?

Martin Armstrong: Inflation starts when people lose faith in government entirely and begin dumping cash for tangible assets. This isn't limited to gold. During hyperinflation in Germany, people bought art, antiques, and real estate—anything tangible.

The next inflationary cycle is forming now, but it will peak around 2024. Expect rising interest rates on the private side, driven by higher inflation expectations.

Kerry Lutz: You've mentioned a bifurcation in interest rates. Can you elaborate?

Martin Armstrong: Absolutely. We're heading toward two distinct interest rate systems.

1. **Government Rates:** Artificially suppressed, manipulated by central banks to keep debt servicing costs low.
2. **Private Sector Rates:** Rising, as lenders demand compensation for inflation and currency risk.

Private interest rates will climb because inflation expectations are rising. Borrowers will have to pay more, especially for consumer credit, even as government rates stay low.

Kerry Lutz: Let's talk about Europe. What's happening there?

Martin Armstrong: Europe is a mess. Between the Islamic immigration crisis, economic stagnation, and ECB policy failures, capital is fleeing to the U.S. The eurozone is politically fractured— Italy, for instance, wants to create a two-tier monetary system.

France's Yellow Vest movement and regional tensions in Germany and Spain show how fragmented the EU has become. The U.S. remains the go-to destination for global capital because there's simply no alternative.

Kerry Lutz: Meanwhile, U.S. stocks keep climbing. Why?

Martin Armstrong: It's simple: capital inflows. People criticize the market's rise without understanding the global context. Investors are parking money in U.S. equities because they've lost faith in other governments and markets.

This is the same phenomenon driving gold. When confidence in government collapses, money moves to perceived safe havens—stocks, metals, real estate. The Dow is likely heading to 35,000 as this trend accelerates.

Kerry Lutz: What about Trump and the 2020 election?

Martin Armstrong: The computer models show a tight race, but Trump is still favored to win. He's an outsider who can't be bought, which resonates with many Americans. The alternative—a career politician—would likely lead to draconian policies and increased government overreach.

Kerry Lutz: Let's pivot to climate issues. You've mentioned global cooling. What's the concern?

Martin Armstrong: Global cooling, not warming, is the real threat. Cooler temperatures shorten growing seasons, leading to food shortages. Historical cooling periods, like the Little Ice Age, have coincided with famine and disease.

Right now, we're seeing unseasonably cold weather disrupting planting in the U.S. and Europe. Grain prices are already rising, and this could worsen if cooling intensifies. Instead of preparing for food shortages, governments are busy pushing a climate change agenda to raise taxes.

Kerry Lutz: How about small businesses and education? What's happening there?

Martin Armstrong: Small businesses are struggling because banks refuse to lend to them. Instead, banks focus on high-interest consumer credit, which is more profitable. Restoring usury laws—capping interest rates—could force banks to support small businesses again.

Education is another problem. Colleges push useless degrees, leaving students with massive debt and no job prospects. Practical apprenticeships, like those in Switzerland, would be far more effective.

Kerry Lutz: So, what's the takeaway for listeners?

Martin Armstrong: The global economy is undergoing a massive shift. Confidence in governments and central banks is eroding. This will lead to higher inflation, rising private interest rates, and continued capital flight to the U.S.

Prepare by diversifying into tangible assets—gold, real estate, or stocks. Watch for geopolitical instability and economic turbulence, especially in Europe. And above all, understand the broader cycles driving these changes.

Kerry Lutz: Great insights, as always, Martin. Thanks for joining us.

Martin Armstrong: My pleasure, Kerry.

Key Takeaways:

1. **Central Banks:** Their policies have failed, eroding confidence in governments.

2. **Inflationary Cycle:** Expected to peak around 2024, driven by mistrust in fiat currencies.

3. **Europe:** Political and economic instability is fueling capital flight to the U.S.

4. **Interest Rates:** A bifurcation is emerging—low government rates vs. rising private rates.

5. **Global Cooling:** Poses significant risks to food supplies and economic stability.

6. **Small Businesses:** Struggling due to a lack of access to affordable credit.

Final Thought:

Armstrong's analysis underscores the importance of understanding economic cycles and positioning accordingly to navigate these turbulent times.

THE GLOBAL ECONOMIC CROSSROADS (NOVEMBER 12, 2019)

Interview Summary:

Martin Armstrong unravels the complexities of the repo market crisis, the structural flaws in the Eurozone, and the looming collapse of socialism as a fiscal model. Touching on global civil unrest, the resilience of the U.S. stock market, and the future of China's economy, Armstrong provides a deep dive into the economic and political dynamics shaping the world.

Kerry Lutz: Welcome to *The Financial Survival Network*. It's November 12, 2019, and we're diving deep into the repo market mess, gold, and the stock market's trajectory with a guest you've been asking to hear from—Martin Armstrong. Martin, it's great to have you back. Crazy world out there.

Martin Armstrong: Thanks for having me. And yes, it's going to get worse.

Kerry Lutz: Just when it feels safe to step outside...

Martin Armstrong: Governments worldwide are proving incapable of meaningful action. We've lost civility across the board. It's not just the U.S.; look at Brexit. The people voted to leave, but for three years, opposition forces obstructed it. Democracy itself is under siege globally.

Kerry Lutz: Let's get into the repo market. What's going on, and why did it suddenly lock up until the Fed intervened?

Martin Armstrong: Ironically, the repo market issues have little to do with the U.S. The root problem lies in Europe and the eurozone's flawed construction. When the euro was created, Germany insisted on no consolidation of debts among member nations.

I warned them at the time that this would lead to disaster. Without a unified debt system, Europe's banking sector became fragmented. Banks hold a mix of state debts, making them vulnerable to regional crises.

Kerry Lutz: How does this tie to Deutsche Bank?

Martin Armstrong: Deutsche Bank is the largest bank in Europe with a massive derivative book that connects it to banks worldwide. If Deutsche Bank collapses, the ripple effects will be catastrophic.

European politicians boxed themselves in with bail-in policies—banks can't be bailed out because that would require cross-border financial support, which is politically unacceptable. This leaves institutions like Deutsche Bank on precarious footing.

U.S. banks, wary of overnight risk, are pulling back from lending in the repo market. The Fed stepped in to fill this gap, not because of domestic issues but to mitigate global risks.

Kerry Lutz: Beyond the financial system, we're seeing societal and fiscal collapses in states like California, Illinois, and New York. What's your perspective?

Martin Armstrong: This is the collapse of socialism. Governments promised benefits—pensions, healthcare—without the fiscal means to sustain them. Unfunded liabilities are projected to reach $400 trillion by 2032.

This "vote for me, and I'll give you XYZ" model is breaking down. Pension funds globally, particularly in Europe, are failing due to negative interest rates and unrealistic return expectations.

Kerry Lutz: Despite all this turmoil, the U.S. stock market keeps breaking records. Why?

Martin Armstrong: Capital inflows. Global investors view the U.S. as a safe haven amidst global instability. The market isn't driven by domestic earnings alone—it's fueled by a lack of alternatives.

The U.S. bond market is unattractive, and gold, while appealing to individuals, isn't viable for institutional investors. Equities remain the best option. This dynamic will continue to push the market higher, with corrections serving as buying opportunities.

Kerry Lutz: Gold has pulled back recently. What's next for precious metals?

Martin Armstrong: Gold's rise depends on a broader collapse in confidence in government. The general public—not just seasoned investors—must recognize the systemic problems.

We've seen moments of panic before, like in the 1980s, but today's younger generation is less inclined toward gold. They're comfortable with digital payments and cryptocurrencies, delaying gold's breakout.

Kerry Lutz: Shifting gears, what about China?

Martin Armstrong: China isn't strictly communist anymore. It's moved toward an authoritarian-managed economy, which allows for long-term planning. This gives it an edge over democracies mired in short-term election cycles.

China is actively developing its domestic economy, reducing reliance on exports. By 2032, China will likely surpass the U.S. as the financial capital of the world, not because of its size alone but due to strategic foresight.

Kerry Lutz: What keeps the U.S. dollar so dominant?

Martin Armstrong: Stability and trust. Unlike other nations, the U.S. has never canceled its currency. About 70% of paper dollars circulate outside the U.S., cementing its role as the global reserve currency.

Europe and other regions routinely cancel currencies, eroding trust. This stark difference underpins the dollar's resilience, even amidst rising U.S. debt levels.

Kerry Lutz: With everything happening, where should people put their money?

Martin Armstrong: The private sector. As governments fail, capital will flow into equities and other private assets. The bond market is increasingly risky, and gold is too small for institutional investors.

Kerry Lutz: Thanks for another enlightening conversation, Martin. For more, visit ArmstrongEconomics.com.

Martin Armstrong: Thank you, Kerry.

Key Takeaways:

1. **Repo Market Crisis:** Rooted in Europe's structural banking flaws and Deutsche Bank's precarious position.
2. **Collapse of Socialism:** Unfunded liabilities and failing pension systems are unsustainable.
3. **U.S. Stock Market:** Driven by global capital inflows as investors seek stability.
4. **Gold's Future:** Hinges on a broader loss of confidence in governments.
5. **China's Strategy:** Focused on long-term domestic growth, poised to lead by 2032.

Final Thought:

This chapter underscores the fragility of global financial systems and the pivotal role of the U.S. in maintaining economic stability amidst rising uncertainty.

MANIPULATING THE WORLD ECONOMY: INSIGHTS FROM MARTIN ARMSTRONG (DECEMBER 19, 2019)

Interview Summary:

Martin Armstrong dives deep into his new book, *Manipulating the World Economy: The Rise of Modern Monetary Theory and the Fall of Classical Economics*. The discussion spans topics like the flaws of economic theories, the velocity of money, global debt crises, and possible solutions for government and private debt. Armstrong highlights his approach to understanding economic cycles and forecasts a significant financial upheaval by 2022.

Kerry Lutz: Welcome back to *The Financial Survival Network*! It's December 19, 2019, and today, we're thrilled to have Martin Armstrong with us to discuss his newly released book, *Manipulating the World Economy*. Martin, it's always a pleasure, and this book is quite a feat. How long did it take you to write it?

Martin Armstrong: Thanks for having me. Honestly, it only took about four to six weeks. It's the culmination of a lifetime of research and experience, so when it came time to write, it all flowed quickly.

Kerry Lutz: What motivated you to write this now?

Martin Armstrong: There's been a growing misunderstanding of modern monetary theory (MMT) and its implications. People see quantitative easing without inflation and assume we can print money indefinitely without consequence. They're missing the larger picture, including the decline in the velocity of money and public confidence in the system.

Kerry Lutz: You emphasize the velocity of money in your book. Can you explain its importance?

Martin Armstrong: The velocity of money measures how quickly money circulates in the economy. When people hoard cash due to uncertainty, velocity drops, and inflation remains subdued despite money printing. Hyperinflation occurs when confidence in the currency collapses, causing people to spend money as fast as they get it.

For example, in the Roman Empire, even debased bronze coins were hoarded because people believed they retained value. In modern times, Europe's negative interest rates have led people to withdraw money from banks and store it in cash.

Kerry Lutz: You critique both Keynesian and Austrian economics. Where do they fall short?

Martin Armstrong: Keynesian economics, derived from Marxist ideas, assumes governments can manipulate the economy successfully. History proves otherwise. The Austrians are closer to the mark but rely on the outdated quantity theory of money.

Modern economic systems have evolved. For example, government debt now acts as collateral in financial systems, effectively making it a form of money. This shift undermines traditional theories.

Kerry Lutz: You propose a debt-to-equity swap as a solution to the global debt crisis. Can you elaborate?

Martin Armstrong: Governments and private entities are drowning in debt. Simply defaulting would destroy pension funds and savings. Instead, we need a structured approach, like Julius Caesar's during Rome's debt crisis, where loans were reassessed based on current values, and past interest payments were forgiven.

A debt-to-equity swap could stabilize economies, with governments prohibited from borrowing in the future. Instead, they'd fund expenditures through controlled money supply growth tied to GDP.

Kerry Lutz: What about student debt? How do we address that?

Martin Armstrong: Student debt is a major problem. Much of it should be forgiven, and the government should exit the loan business. Colleges have inflated costs because they know loans will cover them.

Additionally, the education system fails to teach critical thinking. Degrees often don't translate to viable careers, leaving graduates with unpayable debt. Reform is essential.

Kerry Lutz: You've consistently predicted the stock market's rise when others forecasted crashes. What's your outlook now?

Martin Armstrong: The market is fueled by global capital inflows seeking refuge from instability elsewhere. People are still hoarding cash, but as confidence grows, more money will flow into equities. We're likely to see the Dow reach 40,000 before any major decline.

Kerry Lutz: You mention a significant financial crisis by 2022. What's driving that?

Martin Armstrong: Negative interest rates in Europe, over $17 trillion in negative-yielding bonds, and widespread pension fund insolvency are major risks. The system wasn't designed for these conditions. When the bond bubble bursts, it will trigger a global financial crisis.

Kerry Lutz: What's the best outcome you hope for with your book?

Martin Armstrong: Awareness. Policymakers need to understand the systemic flaws and act before it's too late. The public needs to demand accountability and rational solutions. If nothing changes, the crisis will force action—but at a much higher cost.

Kerry Lutz: *Manipulating the World Economy* is a must-read. Thank you, Martin, for sharing your insights. We'll follow up soon, possibly with a webinar to address listener questions.

Martin Armstrong: Thank you, Kerry.

Key Takeaways:

1. **Velocity of Money:** A critical factor in understanding inflation and economic stability.
2. **Debt-to-Equity Swap:** A practical solution to manage unsustainable government and private debt.
3. **Stock Market Outlook:** Continued growth fueled by global capital inflows.
4. **Student Debt:** Calls for forgiveness and systemic reform.
5. **Future Crisis:** A financial upheaval by 2022 due to systemic risks in bonds and pensions.

Final Thought:

This chapter captures Armstrong's comprehensive approach to economic cycles, his critique of prevailing theories, and his vision for a more stable financial future.

ECONOMIC TURMOIL AND POLITICAL SHIFTS AMIDST COVID-19 (MARCH 17, 2020)

Interview Summary:

Kerry Lutz and Martin Armstrong discuss the unprecedented economic shutdowns sparked by COVID-19, comparing the media-driven frenzy to historical events like the Spanish-American War. Armstrong criticizes the extensive lockdowns, citing low mortality rates compared to the flu, and warns of severe economic consequences, especially for small businesses. They address financial market volatility, driven by liquidity crises and declining confidence in central banks, and predict a temporary downturn in the stock market with a likely recovery over the long term. Armstrong also anticipates a broader move toward digital currencies, particularly in Europe, and the potential elimination of paper money as a government control measure. Armstrong emphasizes the need for confidence to shift back to the private sector for a sustainable economic recovery.

Kerry Lutz: Welcome to *The Financial Survival Network*! Crazy times demand crazy people with crazy solutions, and that's what we're seeing. Martin Armstrong is here from Armstrong Economics to give his perspective. Martin, it's great to have you back. You were just at Mar-a-Lago last week before they shut it down. Now, what's happening with the economy, stock market, and the world?

Martin Armstrong: Well, honestly, the only thing close to this was when Pulitzer and Hearst stirred up the Spanish-American War with fake news. But now the economic damage is far greater. They're causing massive closures, shutting down restaurants, and displacing workers—many of them students. People don't realize the lasting

153

impact; you can't just shut everything down and expect to restart. Less than 8,000 people have died worldwide, and about 200,000 are infected, but we have over 600,000 die from the flu each year. Back in 1968, the worst flu killed 3 million people. Now, we're shutting down the entire global economy over this?

Kerry Lutz: It's extreme. And considering the seasonality, viruses typically decrease with warmer weather. By April or May, odds are high this will fade—80% likely.

Martin Armstrong: Right. Flu season happens in colder weather, not warm. And for those worried about global warming, society actually does better in warmer conditions than in global cooling. China's already seeing fewer cases, and South Korea's numbers are down. The real question is whether this will be a parallel flu next season. But shutting down the whole economy for 8,000 deaths worldwide is an overreaction, and the economic fallout will be severe.

Kerry Lutz: We're even seeing gold crashing. Is that because funds like Bridgewater are getting margin calls?

Martin Armstrong: Yes, hedge funds like Bridgewater are selling to meet those calls. I warned about this at our conference in October; our model showed a downturn starting in January, predicting a crash like 2008 combined with 1998. Back then, long-term capital management had invested in Russian bonds, couldn't find buyers, and had to sell everything. Now, the same thing is happening—gold, Japanese yen—everything's on sale. It's a liquidity crisis, plain and simple.

Kerry Lutz: The stock market is tanking. Once this madness subsides, do you see recovery, or did this just kick off a prolonged bear market?

Martin Armstrong: No, I think it will recover, eventually reaching new highs. People are starting to lose confidence in government. I put out a report on the central bank crisis; the Fed went all-in with rate cuts, and the market called their bluff. Now confidence in government is eroding. In 1980, gold went up because people lost confidence in government, and we're moving toward that again. The Fed's done everything it can, and there's nothing more they can do. Negative interest rates haven't worked in Europe—they've destroyed the economy there.

Kerry Lutz: You met Trump recently. What's your take on him?

Martin Armstrong: I've met many presidents. Trump, unlike career politicians, will change his mind. If something isn't working, he'll adjust, unlike politicians who stick to their stance even if it leads to disaster. Career politicians won't admit mistakes. Trump at least gives you an honest read on what he thinks.

Kerry Lutz: He's unpredictable but not afraid to shift course. What about the election? Will Biden be the nominee, or will someone else step in?

Martin Armstrong: Behind the scenes, the word is that Biden's dealing with health issues, likely dementia. They pushed him up to block Bernie, but there's no way he'll get enough votes on the first ballot. So, they're planning to draft Hillary. That's why she's making appearances. The feeling is that she can beat Trump, while Biden and Bernie can't.

Kerry Lutz: Interesting. But a Midwest governor might be a safer choice since they need states like Pennsylvania and Michigan. The Bernie or bust voters won't rally for Hillary.

Martin Armstrong: They still think Hillary can win, though our models don't show it. But yes, their options are limited.

Kerry Lutz: Back to financial matters—are we heading for a depression, or is this a temporary downturn?

Martin Armstrong: I think Trump is the best choice right now because we're heading toward a real monetary crisis. In Europe, there's talk of eliminating paper currency under the guise that it spreads the virus. Some coffee shops in Canada and stores in Illinois have already stopped accepting cash. It's a push to go digital so central banks can control everything. Keynesian economics is dead; their only tool left is authoritarianism. The argument is that without cash, people can't hoard, and there would be no bank runs. But this is a power grab.

Kerry Lutz: What about stock market predictions? Is there a rough patch ahead, or are we seeing a slow recovery?

Martin Armstrong: If Tuesday closes higher than Monday, we might see a bounce, but another dip could come by early April. Worst case, we might test 19,000 on the Dow before things stabilize. The quarter's end could bring more liquidation across assets. Right now, it's all about cash. That's where Bridgewater got it wrong. The business cycle always wins. Once confidence returns to the private sector, we'll see equities and gold rise, but that shift in confidence has to happen first.

Kerry Lutz: So, in the long run, you think we'll surpass 30,000 again?

Martin Armstrong: Absolutely. Long-term, nothing's changed. The Dow could reach 40,000 by 2022 or 2024 and potentially 65,000 by 2032. But keep in mind, we may also see digital currencies taking over, especially in Europe. That could add new layers to the financial landscape.

Kerry Lutz: Incredible times. Go check out Armstrong Economics and sign up for their newsletter. Martin, thanks as always for the insights.

Martin Armstrong: Thanks for having me, Kerry. Always a pleasure.

Key Takeaways:

1. **COVID-19 Overreaction:** Armstrong argues the pandemic's response is disproportionate given its mortality rates compared to historical pandemics.
2. **Liquidity Crisis:** Financial volatility stems from a liquidity crunch, with investors selling assets like gold to cover margin calls.
3. **Digital Currency Push:** COVID-19 is accelerating moves toward digital currencies, particularly in Europe, with concerns over government control.
4. **Stock Market Recovery:** Armstrong predicts a recovery in equities and the Dow surpassing 30,000 in the long run, despite near-term turbulence.
5. **Confidence in the Private Sector:** Restoring confidence in the private sector is essential for sustainable economic recovery.

Final Thought:

Martin Armstrong highlights the dangers of overreaction to COVID-19, emphasizing the need to maintain economic stability. His long-term outlook underscores the importance of private sector confidence, cautioning against government overreach as the world grapples with unprecedented challenges.

Economic Uncertainty and Global Shifts Amidst a Pandemic (June 17, 2020)

Interview Summary:

Kerry Lutz and Martin Armstrong discuss the ongoing economic impacts of COVID-19 and the shifts in global power dynamics. Armstrong explains how the pandemic has exacerbated underlying economic weaknesses, especially in Europe, and accelerated trends like the shift toward digital currencies and centralized control. They delve into the U.S. stock market's unpredictable recovery, the future of inflation driven by monetary policy, and the tensions within Europe and between global powers like the U.S., China, and Russia. Armstrong predicts that as governments continue to struggle to manage the crisis, people's confidence will move back toward tangible assets and private sector investments.

Kerry Lutz: Welcome to *The Financial Survival Network*! Joining us again is Martin Armstrong from Armstrong Economics. It's been a few months since we last spoke, and the world's still reeling. Martin, thanks for being here. What's happening with the economy and global markets right now?

Martin Armstrong: Great to be here, Kerry. Well, what we're seeing is a complete shift in global economic dynamics. COVID-19 didn't create these issues but accelerated existing trends and weaknesses, especially in Europe. They were already struggling with debt and negative interest rates, and now they're facing even more challenges.

Kerry Lutz: We're hearing talk about digital currencies more and more. Do you think COVID-19 is pushing governments toward digital control?

Martin Armstrong: Absolutely. The move to digital currencies is very much tied to controlling the economy and tracking every transaction. Central banks, especially in Europe, see this as an answer to their problems. They can eliminate cash, which prevents people from hoarding money outside the system. That way, they can keep interest rates low or even negative without worrying that people will withdraw cash.

Kerry Lutz: And what's the endgame there?

Martin Armstrong: Ultimately, it's about control. When cash is eliminated, governments can dictate every financial move. If you have to keep your money in the bank, they can impose negative rates or restrictions on spending. Europe's pushing hard on this idea, but it's getting some resistance here in the U.S., which is good.

Kerry Lutz: Turning to the stock market, we saw an impressive recovery, but is it sustainable?

Martin Armstrong: We're seeing an artificial bounce fueled by liquidity injections from the Fed. But this isn't a real economic recovery. Businesses are still struggling, especially small businesses, which employ a huge portion of the population. So, while the stock market might look good on paper, the underlying economy is far from stable.

Kerry Lutz: It sounds like you're saying this is more of a liquidity-driven rally.

Martin Armstrong: Exactly. Liquidity-driven markets can't be sustained forever. The real economy is not improving as fast as the stock market. The longer the Fed props it up, the more likely we'll see inflation down the line because there's so much money in circulation without corresponding productivity.

Kerry Lutz: Do you see inflation becoming a major issue soon?

Martin Armstrong: Yes, especially in commodities and tangible assets. People are losing confidence in traditional assets and are looking at gold, real estate, and other physical assets. Inflation will show up here first because these are viewed as safe havens.

Kerry Lutz: So, the traditional safe havens still hold value?

Martin Armstrong: Yes, especially in times like these. We're already seeing a rise in real estate prices, particularly in places like Florida, as people flee high-tax states. Gold's also holding its value. People are trying to secure their wealth outside the banking system because they don't trust governments and central banks to keep things stable.

Kerry Lutz: With governments taking more control and people turning to alternative assets, what does that mean for the future of fiat currency?

Martin Armstrong: The trend toward digital currency is, in a way, governments' attempt to keep control of fiat currency. They're worried people will shift to alternative assets, which weakens their grip on the economy. We might see more pressure to adopt digital currencies or even a global currency if this trend continues.

Kerry Lutz: You mentioned Europe's struggles—how serious are they?

Martin Armstrong: Europe is in a tough spot. They're facing negative interest rates, high debt levels, and no real way to stimulate the economy. Some are talking about outright nationalization of industries as a last resort. This isn't a healthy system. The euro's losing ground because people are looking at the U.S. dollar and even gold as more stable.

Kerry Lutz: And with the U.S., we're not exactly on solid ground, either.

Martin Armstrong: True, but the U.S. has more flexibility than Europe. The Fed has room to maneuver compared to the ECB. Plus, the U.S. dollar is still the reserve currency, so there's more demand. However, if the dollar continues to weaken or inflation picks up too fast, that could change. The U.S. can't afford to rest easy.

Kerry Lutz: What about global tensions with countries like China and Russia? Are they impacting this crisis?

Martin Armstrong: Absolutely. China and Russia are watching how the West handles this crisis, and they're making their moves. China is pushing its influence globally, particularly in Asia, and Russia's focused on its regional influence. COVID-19 is just another factor pushing these powers to consolidate and strengthen their positions. This isn't just about economics; it's about who has the upper hand globally.

Kerry Lutz: Do you think we'll see more conflicts or a power struggle?

Martin Armstrong: It's likely. We're already seeing signs of this in areas like trade and technology. China and Russia are looking for ways to reduce their dependency on the U.S. and Europe. If tensions continue, we could see economic and even military posturing as each side tries to gain leverage.

Kerry Lutz: So, in the next few years, where does this leave the average person trying to preserve their wealth?

Martin Armstrong: Focus on tangible assets and consider alternatives to cash. Real estate, gold, even collectibles are good options. These assets hold value when confidence in government and fiat currency is low. The best thing to do right now is to stay flexible, keep informed, and be prepared for a changing economy.

Kerry Lutz: Thanks, Martin. As always, great insights. And for everyone listening, head over to Armstrong Economics for more.

Martin Armstrong: Thanks for having me, Kerry. Always a pleasure.

Key Takeaways:

1. **Pandemic Accelerating Trends:** COVID-19 has fast-tracked existing economic weaknesses and the move toward centralized digital currencies.
2. **Liquidity-Driven Recovery:** The U.S. stock market recovery is artificial, fueled by the Fed, with underlying economic weaknesses still prevalent.
3. **Inflation and Safe Havens:** Inflation will likely rise in tangible assets like gold and real estate, which are viewed as more secure.
4. **Europe's Struggles:** Negative interest rates and debt are eroding Europe's financial stability, with the euro losing favor.
5. **Global Tensions:** Rising tensions between global powers could lead to economic and geopolitical shifts, impacting trade and security.

Final Thought:

Martin Armstrong's insights underscore the importance of tangible assets and staying adaptable in a volatile global economy. As governments grapple with control and crises deepen, individuals must remain informed and proactive to navigate the uncertainty ahead.

ELECTION 2020 AND THE GLOBAL ECONOMIC CRISIS (OCTOBER 20, 2020)

Interview Summary:

In this discussion, Kerry Lutz and Martin Armstrong tackle the anticipated turmoil surrounding the 2020 U.S. presidential election. Armstrong's forecasting model predicts a tight popular vote, but with an Electoral College edge for Trump. The discussion highlights growing corruption and instability, the implications of foreign influence, and systemic issues in Washington. Armstrong explores the consequences of worldwide economic shifts exacerbated by the pandemic, government debt, and the anticipated rise of digital currencies. Social unrest, a potential sovereign debt crisis, and the economic aftermath of the pandemic indicate turbulent times ahead. Armstrong also shares thoughts on potential global economic and political shifts, suggesting that America and other nations brace for profound, ongoing changes.

Kerry Lutz: Welcome to *The Financial Survival Network*. Today is 10-20-20. The election is right around the corner, and who better to talk to than Martin Armstrong from ArmstrongEconomics.com. Martin has been involved in so many transitions in our monetary system and paid the price for it too. Great to have you back on, Martin. What's your election prediction and the impact on the economy?

Martin Armstrong: Well, I can say this. The popular vote looks tight, almost a 50-50 split. In the Electoral College, our model shows Trump should win, with a voter turnout likely around 55 to 61 percent. Our model has never been wrong, but remember it also predicted that Gore should have won before the Supreme Court gave it to Bush. This election, which our model has said since 1985 would be the most corrupt in American history, is showing just that. You've got all the tech companies conspiring; it's a complete mess. With all the mail-in ballots, I don't think we'll know who the president is until at least two weeks post-election, maybe even December.

Kerry Lutz: Biden revelations are out, showing him like a political crime family boss. Does that matter?

Martin Armstrong: That's standard in Washington. Remember when Hillary was dealing with Haiti? They gave a mining contract to her brother, who wasn't even a miner. You only need to disclose your spouse, so any money going to family is fair game. This isn't just Biden; it's standard practice across parties.

Kerry Lutz: Many politicians are compromised, it seems, with connections to our adversaries.

Martin Armstrong: Exactly. That's why I'm against career politicians. It was one of Trump's campaign points, though I wasn't sure he'd succeed because no one's going to vote themselves out. There's no stability here, and this election cycle is like a yo-yo, with major economic impacts and constant policy changes.

Kerry Lutz: So, long-term impact of the pandemic on the economy, here and globally?

Martin Armstrong: We're showing the economy won't bottom until about 2022. They've created an economic disruption on a global scale. Look at Thailand, which is mainly tourism-dependent, with only 58 deaths in a population of 69 million. People worldwide are starting to protest, but social media is silencing it. Amazon's even canceling books. It's gone too far.

Kerry Lutz: The pandemic seems man-made and unnecessary.

Martin Armstrong: Yes, Florida's open, but elsewhere, restrictions are intense. I bought a box of masks from Amazon, and right on it, it says it won't prevent any disease. But if you're caught without a mask in France three times, you go to prison. It's clear there's another agenda, possibly tied to climate change. The WHO director even mentioned climate change in his discussions.

Kerry Lutz: So, socialists, climate change activists, and population control advocates are working together?

Martin Armstrong: Yes, and they're also eyeing digital currency, possibly by January 1 in Europe. They want to control all transactions globally. Facebook and Twitter have been sanctioning Trump but not Biden—it's clear they've been bought into this agenda.

Kerry Lutz: So, what should the average person do? What about investing?

Martin Armstrong: After an 11-year stock market rally, we're due for a two-year correction. If Trump wins, we could see a rally into 2022, mainly due to capital fleeing other areas. It's less about the economy being strong and more about capital moving globally. We foresee a peak around 2033, with commodities rising between 2022 and 2024, especially due to supply chain issues and some bad weather.

Kerry Lutz: What about the blue wave Wall Street's pitching as bullish?

Martin Armstrong: If they get a blue wave, we could see extreme economic policies like tax increases. The markets might rise for a bit but are due for a correction. The Democrats won't hold control past 2022, which suggests they'll push drastic measures that could backfire economically.

Kerry Lutz: It sounds like there's chaos and economic instability.

Martin Armstrong: Definitely. California's new rule that all cars must be electric by 2035 is unrealistic—they're already facing rolling blackouts. Lockdowns have decreased oil demand, and they're using this as an excuse to push climate agendas, costing jobs globally.

Kerry Lutz: Can Trump's reelection solve any of this, or is it just a delay?

Martin Armstrong: Just a delay. Many politicians signed onto this nonsense because we're facing a monetary and sovereign debt crisis. Since 2014, negative interest rates have failed to stimulate the economy. ECB, Bank of Japan—they're stuck. Interest rates can't rise without risking collapse, so they're stuck buying government bonds that no one else wants.

Key Takeaways:

1. **Election Uncertainty:** Armstrong predicts a tight popular vote with Trump leading in the Electoral College but warns of delays and disputes over results.
2. **Pandemic Fallout:** The global economy faces long-term disruption, with recovery not expected until 2022. Lockdowns have exacerbated economic and social instability.
3. **Digital Currencies:** Governments are pushing digital currencies to control transactions, with Europe eyeing implementation by January 2021.
4. **Investment Outlook:** A stock market correction is likely after the 11-year rally, but Trump's win could delay this until 2022. Commodities are expected to rise between 2022 and 2024.
5. **Global Policy Shifts:** Political agendas are driving economic instability, with climate-related initiatives and energy policies creating further challenges.

Final Thought:

Martin Armstrong emphasizes the need for vigilance and adaptability as the world navigates political, economic, and social upheavals. Preparing for long-term shifts and understanding global trends are essential in safeguarding individual financial stability amid uncertain times.

THE 2020 ELECTION, THE GREAT RESET, AND THE FUTURE OF CAPITALISM (NOVEMBER 20, 2020)

Interview Summary:

In this installment of *The Financial Survival Network*, host Kerry Lutz discusses the tumultuous post-election landscape with Martin Armstrong. They explore allegations of fraud, the implications of a potential Biden presidency, and the larger agenda of the so-called Great Reset. Topics include the collapse of small businesses, shifts in the global financial system, the potential elimination of physical currencies, and threats to capitalism itself.

Kerry Lutz: Welcome to *The Financial Survival Network*. Things are crazy out there—recounts, allegations of fraud, and widespread confusion. Are we all being gaslighted? Martin Armstrong from *Armstrong Economics* is here to help us make sense of it. Martin, where do we stand?

Martin Armstrong: Thanks, Kerry. To be frank, this election is the most corrupt in American history, even beyond what I anticipated. Our computer models flagged it early on. What we're witnessing isn't just a battle between Democrats and Republicans—this is part of a global agenda.

Pelosi has already declared a Biden victory as a mandate to overhaul the economy. What's behind this? The Great Reset. The driving force is the collapse of socialism.

Kerry Lutz: Socialism? Isn't capitalism under fire right now?

Martin Armstrong: It's socialism that's failing. Their programs— pensions, welfare, state-run industries—are unfunded and unsustainable. In Europe, the ECB took interest rates negative in 2014, buying government bonds to prop up the system. Yet, it's failed to stimulate real economic growth.

Now, they're turning to what I call *Communism 3.0*. Schwab's World Economic Forum openly promotes the idea: "You'll own nothing, and you'll be happy." It's not capitalism that's collapsing but their socialist structures.

Kerry Lutz: What about the lockdowns and their economic impact?

Martin Armstrong: The lockdowns are deliberate, aimed at destroying small businesses—the backbone of capitalism. It's like Marxism all over again. The bourgeoisie (small business owners) are demonized. Hospitality, travel, and retail industries have been decimated.

In places like New York City and London, we've seen third-generation shops shut down permanently. A third of businesses in London are already gone, and it's only going to get worse. This is part of a larger agenda to centralize control and wealth.

Kerry Lutz: What's next for currency? Is a digital dollar on the horizon?

Martin Armstrong: Absolutely. The Democrats already have a proposal for a digital dollar in Congress. Foreign governments are lobbying for it too. Europe plans to eliminate physical euros, and the only way to counter hoarded U.S. dollars is for the U.S. to follow suit.

They've weaponized the pandemic, claiming cash spreads COVID, to push this agenda. If Biden takes office, expect moves toward digital currency, which will give governments total control over financial transactions.

Kerry Lutz: What does this mean for gold, silver, and cryptocurrencies?

Martin Armstrong: Gold and silver may see increased demand as people hedge against government overreach. However, I'd caution where you store it. Look at what happened during the 1930s: gold held in banks was confiscated.

Cryptocurrencies like Bitcoin are also under threat. Governments hate competition, and they'll likely seize or regulate crypto assets, converting them into their digital currencies.

Kerry Lutz: This election seems to have deepened divisions in the U.S. Could it lead to civil unrest?

Martin Armstrong: Unfortunately, yes. The U.S. is as divided now as it was during the Civil War. We're seeing ideological splits that could escalate into conflict. If the Democrats gain full control, they'll likely use emergency powers to delay or even cancel future elections.

Our models show rising political turbulence through 2024. By 2022, we could see significant unrest, potentially even a push for secession in some regions.

Kerry Lutz: Is this the end of capitalism as we know it?

Martin Armstrong: If the Great Reset succeeds, yes. Their plan is to shift everything to government control—property, wealth, even debt. Schwab's agenda is about eliminating private ownership under the guise of debt forgiveness.

This isn't the first time we've seen such moves. Under communism, small businesses and private farms were destroyed. The result? Starvation and economic collapse.

Kerry Lutz: Any hope for those of us who value freedom and free markets?

Martin Armstrong: The fight isn't over. Awareness is key. People need to understand the agenda behind these policies. Events like the *World Economic Forum* in December will shed light on these issues.

Kerry Lutz: Martin, your insights are invaluable. Let's hope we can counter this madness. Thanks for joining us.

Martin Armstrong: Thanks, Kerry. See you in Orlando for the forum.

Key Takeaways:

1. **Election Integrity:** Allegations of fraud have sparked a crisis of confidence in democracy.
2. **The Great Reset:** A global push to centralize control under the guise of addressing climate change and inequality.
3. **Economic Impact:** Small businesses are the primary casualties of lockdowns and restrictive policies.
4. **Digital Currency:** Governments are moving to eliminate physical cash, paving the way for digital currencies.
5. **Civil Unrest:** The deepening political divide in the U.S. could lead to significant unrest by 2022.

Final Thought:

Armstrong's analysis underscores the urgent need for vigilance and proactive measures to safeguard individual freedoms and market systems amidst a rapidly changing global landscape.

The Cycle of War and the Coronavirus: Insights from Martin Armstrong (February 13, 2021)

Interview Summary:

In this episode of *The Financial Survival Network*, Martin Armstrong discusses his new book, *The Cycle of War and the Coronavirus*. The conversation spans the global economic and societal impacts of COVID-19, the Great Reset, rising inflation driven by shortages, and systemic risks in Western economies. Armstrong also explores how history informs current crises and forecasts significant political and economic turbulence in the near future.

Kerry Lutz: Welcome back to *The Financial Survival Network*. Today, we have a real treat: Martin Armstrong is here to talk about his latest book, *The Cycle of War and the Coronavirus*. Martin, it's always great to have you. Let's dive right in. Is there anywhere in the world we can escape what's coming?

Martin Armstrong: Thanks, Kerry. Honestly, no. Asia might fare better—China, for instance, posted a 4% growth rate in 2020 compared to the near 10% decline in Britain. But globally, the West has gone off the rails, largely driven by agendas like those of the World Economic Forum (WEF). The "Build Back Better" slogan, used by leaders worldwide, is part of a coordinated agenda that's reshaping society and not necessarily for the better.

Kerry Lutz: What's your take on the WEF and the so-called Great Reset?

Martin Armstrong: The Great Reset, as proposed by Klaus Schwab and others, is a top-down attempt to reshape the world. They're pushing green agendas by destroying industries they consider "non-green," with little regard for the people affected. Coal miners, for instance, are told to learn solar panel manufacturing as if those jobs are readily available.

The problem with these policies is their detachment from reality. Schwab's ideas, like stakeholder economics, date back to the 1930s and don't make sense in today's context. Their plans are elitist and ignore the practicalities of how societies function.

Kerry Lutz: How does inflation fit into all this?

Martin Armstrong: Inflation is coming, but not in the traditional sense. It's driven by shortages rather than monetary expansion. The pandemic disrupted supply chains—crops rotted in fields, factories closed, and goods became scarce.

For example, I bought a refrigerator in December, but it won't be delivered until March because the chips come from Thailand. As shortages worsen, people will pay more to secure goods sooner, driving up prices. This dynamic is set to peak around 2024.

Kerry Lutz: You've talked about a crisis of confidence in governments. How does that play out?

Martin Armstrong: Historically, when confidence in governments collapses, people start abandoning traditional currencies and institutions. Take Rome—Emperor Valerian I was captured and enslaved by the Persians, which shattered public trust.

Today, we see a similar erosion of trust. The pandemic highlighted government failures, and confidence is plummeting. This is when assets like gold and silver become appealing—not because of inflation, but because people lose faith in governments.

Kerry Lutz: What's your view on the recent short squeezes, like GameStop?

Martin Armstrong: While short squeezes are nothing new, the GameStop saga highlights problems with high-frequency trading and naked short selling. These tactics amplify volatility and create risks. The Redditors made a point, but the real issue lies in how financial systems have evolved to favor insiders.

Kerry Lutz: What about the stock market? Can it keep going up as the economy struggles?

Martin Armstrong: Yes, for now. Capital has to go somewhere, and with bond markets unattractive, equities are the primary option. Big money can't move into gold or silver at scale, so it flows into stocks.

Our models show the Dow reaching 35,000 in the near term, and potentially 65,000 by 2030. It's not about fundamentals but a lack of alternatives.

Kerry Lutz: Schwab's vision for 2030 includes the idea that "you'll own nothing and be happy." What does that mean?

Martin Armstrong: Schwab's proposal essentially advocates for governments to default on their debts by forgiving personal debts like mortgages and student loans. They'll frame it as a benefit to the people, but in reality, it's a coordinated default on public and private debt.

This approach is fundamentally flawed. It ignores who owns the debt—mainly pension funds and retirees. Wiping out debt would destroy the financial security of millions.

Kerry Lutz: Is there any hope for U.S. politics? Could Trump return, Grover Cleveland-style?

Martin Armstrong: Trump could create a third party, but systemic issues in elections make real reform unlikely. Both major parties are fractured—the Democrats have a divide between moderates and the far left, and Republicans are split over Trump.

Our models show political chaos peaking in 2022, potentially leading to the formation of new political movements. A third party could attract conservatives from both parties, but it's unclear if that would resolve the underlying issues.

Kerry Lutz: Martin, your insights are always fascinating. Any closing thoughts?

Martin Armstrong: The world is at a tipping point. Confidence in governments is eroding, and we're seeing the consequences in markets, inflation, and societal unrest. My advice is to stay informed and prepared—this isn't over yet.

Kerry Lutz: *The Cycle of War and the Coronavirus* is a must-read. Go to Amazon or ArmstrongEconomics.com to get your copy. Thanks, Martin.

Martin Armstrong: Thanks, Kerry. Take care.

Key Takeaways:

1. **Inflationary Pressures**: Driven by shortages rather than monetary policy.
2. **The Great Reset**: A top-down agenda with significant risks to economic stability and personal freedoms.
3. **Political Chaos**: Expected to peak in 2022, potentially leading to new political movements.
4. **Stock Market Outlook**: Continued growth driven by capital inflows, not fundamentals.
5. **Debt Solutions**: Radical proposals like the Great Reset risk destabilizing financial systems further.

Final Thought:

Armstrong's insights offer a sobering perspective on global trends, emphasizing the importance of understanding history to navigate the present and future.

ECONOMIC AND POLITICAL SHIFTS IN A POST-PANDEMIC WORLD (APRIL 13, 2021)

Interview Summary:

Kerry Lutz and Martin Armstrong explore the turbulent economic and political landscape in the wake of COVID-19, focusing on digital currency, economic instability, and geopolitical concerns. Armstrong discusses the economic manipulation stemming from the pandemic, noting that the virus has been used to push political agendas, including climate policy. He explores inflation's trajectory, the regulatory scrutiny on cryptocurrencies, and the capital flows favoring U.S. markets amid European turmoil. Armstrong predicts rising gold prices with increasing geopolitical tensions and anticipates further exodus from major cities as remote work and high taxes drive migration to low-tax states like Florida. He also highlights the constraints on the judiciary system and concerns about inflation due to supply chain disruptions and government spending.

Kerry Lutz: Welcome to *The Financial Survival Network*. With us is our good friend Martin Armstrong. Martin, it's been a while, great to have you back on the show.

Martin Armstrong: Thanks. Yes, very interesting times indeed—like the old Chinese curse.

Kerry Lutz: Yes, the "curse" feels real. How long can this insanity continue before we either destroy everything or come to our senses?

Martin Armstrong: Well, our computer models have forecasted political shifts using economic trends. When economies decline sharply, you get political change, like in 1929–1932. It's not hard to see: the polls are manipulated. We rely on the economics, and our computer is projecting what we call a "panic cycle" in politics, something we haven't seen since the 1930s. Biden doesn't have a strong mandate, and much of this agenda is coming from overseas.

We started seeing unusual capital flows back in August 2019, and by December 2019, we saw Bill Gates selling stock. By January, some sources were already aware of a virus. The World Economic Forum's "Build Back Better" slogan was also already being discussed. The virus isn't some biological weapon; its death toll is around 0.028%, comparable to the Hong Kong flu of the 1960s. The Spanish flu, by comparison, had a death rate of about 3%—this isn't in that league. But this virus is being used for political purposes, mainly to push climate change agendas.

Kerry Lutz: And on that front, it seems the U.S. is pushing Ukraine to confront Russia over Crimea as a way to justify shutting down that controversial pipeline.

Martin Armstrong: Exactly. It's like what they're doing with pipelines in the U.S.—gasoline prices are rising as a result. In Europe, it's become totalitarian. France is locked down again, stopping short-term flights. A friend in Spain had to get police approval just to travel from Barcelona to Madrid for a meeting, and everything was monitored. I don't see myself returning to Europe soon; it's almost unrecognizable.

Kerry Lutz: It's shocking. What's happening with gold, silver, and cryptocurrencies amid this turmoil?

Martin Armstrong: Cryptocurrency, to an extent, was propagated by governments to acclimate people to digital currency. Once they establish their own digital currencies, they're not going to allow competition. I wouldn't be surprised if they force people to swap their crypto for government-issued currency and ban independent currencies. Historically, no government has allowed a competing currency.

Kerry Lutz: And if the government decides to outlaw Bitcoin, how would people handle it?

Martin Armstrong: In Europe, our Bitcoin report itself was restricted—banks wouldn't accept credit card payments if it involved Bitcoin in any way. If we couldn't sell a report, you can imagine the future regulations around actual cryptocurrency ownership. This could end up like marijuana legalization, where the federal government seizes cash from dispensaries. It's a strange world we're in.

Kerry Lutz: So, when do you see gold and silver rallying, especially with geopolitical tensions rising?

Martin Armstrong: I think May could be a turning point. If you look at 1980, the last major rally to $875 an ounce was when Russia invaded Afghanistan. We might see something similar if geopolitical tensions escalate. Russia has about 80,000 troops on the Ukraine border. This is serious. If I were China, I'd wait until the U.S. was distracted by Russia and then move on Taiwan.

Kerry Lutz: May sounds like a pivotal time. Do you see an inevitability in this escalation?

Martin Armstrong: Yes. May is the strongest target our model has identified for this year, likely due to geopolitical issues.

Kerry Lutz: What price levels could gold reach?

Martin Armstrong: It's hard to say, but gold is highly monitored. Refineries have to report every gram that comes in and where it goes. If they're tracking gold so closely as an alternative asset, you can bet they'll regulate or even confiscate cryptocurrency when they roll out their digital currency.

Kerry Lutz: Crypto advocates argue that governments can't shut down decentralized networks.

Martin Armstrong: The government can certainly try. They know where the nodes are and could target them, whether physically or through cyberattacks.

Kerry Lutz: Speaking of government control, you've often mentioned that the markets are still heading higher. Are we near the end of the rally, or will liquidity continue to prop it up?

Martin Armstrong: We're reaching our first target around 35,000–37,000 on the Dow, with the next target at 65,000 by 2032. Typically, we'd expect a correction, but if geopolitical tensions escalate, capital will flow to the U.S., supporting our markets. This is what made the U.S. the world's financial capital after World Wars I and II, as capital moved here. We're seeing it again with the influx into Florida real estate. I spoke to a realtor who says cash offers are the new norm, even on million-dollar homes. People from New York are buying at double last year's prices.

Kerry Lutz: It's surprising. Cities seem to be emptying out, with people migrating to suburbs and states with no income tax.

Martin Armstrong: Yes, our model predicted migration from cities to suburbs, initially due to tax differences. Now, COVID has accelerated it. Governments think higher populations mean higher revenues, but they ignore the cost of governing larger cities. They've raised property taxes to compensate for fewer businesses, but that just drives more people out. It's a classic public-to-private wave.

Kerry Lutz: And with remote work, many people don't need to stay in high-tax cities.

Martin Armstrong: Exactly. If work is remote, why stay and pay high taxes? I know a top mergers and acquisitions banker who moved here, saying he can work remotely and avoid New York taxes. Even lawyers who traditionally needed to be in New York can now handle cases remotely, and tech companies are telling employees they may never have to return to the office.

Kerry Lutz: It's a major shift. What about inflation? Is it finally catching up?

Martin Armstrong: Yes, inflation is here, especially in commodities. The key isn't just the money supply but also the psychology—people realize it's cheaper to buy today than tomorrow. Prices are up in food, lumber, and construction as people expand homes. Contractors here in Tampa are fully booked. Our model has forecast an inflationary wave, but it's driven by shortages rather than speculation. COVID disrupted supply chains, and now we're seeing prices soar as a result.

Kerry Lutz: Shortages in the supply chain seem pervasive. Even appliances are back-ordered for months.

Martin Armstrong: Yes, and that's contributing to inflation. Supply chains are global—chips for appliances from Thailand, lumber from Canada, and COVID restrictions have disrupted everything. This is what our model predicted: inflation driven by shortages heading into 2024.

Kerry Lutz: It's all starting to unfold. If people want to stay updated, they should head over to ArmstrongEconomics.com. Martin, it's remarkable to see your predictions, like Dow 35,000, coming true, and it looks like gold could surge with tensions rising globally.

Martin Armstrong: Yes, China's crackdown on Hong Kong foreshadows Taiwan's future. I doubt the U.S. will intervene militarily. The Democrats are currently focused on climate change, which drives much of the anti-Russia stance, aiming to stop Russian pipelines into Europe. But this could turn into something much bigger.

Kerry Lutz: Economics always drive politics eventually, as you've often said. Thanks for the insights, Martin, and I hope people sign up for your daily missives. It's always a pleasure having you on.

Martin Armstrong: Thank you for having me, Kerry. Good to see you're doing well.

Key Takeaways:

1. **Digital Currencies and Regulation:** Armstrong predicts governments will eventually regulate or ban independent cryptocurrencies to pave the way for government-controlled digital currencies.
2. **Geopolitical Tensions:** Rising tensions between Russia, Ukraine, and China over Taiwan could create volatility in gold and financial markets.
3. **Inflation Driven by Shortages:** COVID-induced supply chain disruptions have led to inflation, particularly in commodities and construction materials.
4. **Migration and Remote Work:** High taxes and remote work are driving people from major cities to low-tax states like Florida.
5. **Economic Trends:** Armstrong forecasts a rise in the Dow, with geopolitical concerns and capital inflows into the U.S. supporting markets.

Final Thought:

Martin Armstrong underscores the importance of understanding macroeconomic and geopolitical dynamics in navigating the post-pandemic world. The interplay of digital currencies, inflation, and global tensions points to significant long-term shifts, requiring careful planning and adaptability.

THE MOST HATED BULL MARKET IN HISTORY (AUGUST 10, 2021)

Interview Summary:

Martin Armstrong discusses the current state of global economics and politics, analyzing the Great Reset, U.S. and European economic policies, cryptocurrency trends, and the challenges posed by centralized governance. Highlighting the inefficiencies of modern monetary theories and the dangers of consolidating power within unelected institutions like the United Nations and the IMF, Armstrong warns against losing sovereignty and freedoms. He also examines the impacts of hyperinflation, government overreach, and the ongoing shifts in global power dynamics.

Kerry Lutz: It's 8/10/21. We've got a special treat for you today. If you've been following this person like I have for well over a decade and you compare his record of forecast with virtually anyone else out there, his record speaks for itself. When I first interviewed you, Marty, your prognostication was Dow 35,000. I think the Dow was at 14,000 at the time. It's just hit 35,000. Took a little longer, but talk about a bull market that everyone loves to hate.

Martin Armstrong: This is it. The most hated bull market in history. You've called it. There's more to come. You have a lot of other things to say. If you want to follow Marty and find out his latest work, visit ArmstrongEconomics.com. Marty, welcome back. I remember Laurel and Hardy, when Oliver would look at Laurel and say, "It's another fine mess you've gotten me into." Well, we're in a fine mess here in this country, in this world, aren't we?

Armstrong: Oh, that's probably an understatement. What people have to understand is that over the years, I've dealt with probably more governments than anybody else in the analytical field. For decades, I've warned them about the dangers of borrowing year after year with no intention of paying it back. Their response was always, "We're the government. It doesn't apply to us."

Back during the Reagan period, when Volcker raised interest rates to 17%, I met with the Treasury and warned them that the national debt would more than double within a decade just on interest expenditures. They brushed it off, saying, "We'll be paying it back with cheaper dollars." Back then, the national debt was $1 trillion. Now, we're dealing with consequences they can no longer ignore.

Host: What's the broader issue here?

Armstrong: The problem isn't the U.S. so much as Europe. The Federal Reserve, at least, avoided going to negative interest rates. Europe, on the other hand, embraced negative rates in 2014. Seven years later, it has failed to stimulate their economy, destroyed their bond markets, and rendered pension funds insolvent.

Enter Klaus Schwab and the Great Reset. Schwab's agenda for 2030 openly declares that the U.S. will no longer be a superpower, democracy will be replaced with governance by unelected authorities, and power will be handed to the United Nations. This is his vision of a one-world government, supported by figures like George Soros.

Host: What does that mean for the economy?

Armstrong: Schwab and his allies see no problem with defaulting on government debt to achieve this vision. They've already destroyed the bond markets in Europe. Since 2014, governments have been buying their own bonds to fund deficits, creating the illusion that this won't cause inflation. This gave rise to Modern Monetary Theory (MMT), which suggests governments can print unlimited money without consequence.

Host: Is there a way out?

Armstrong: We're heading toward 2032, where governments will face a breaking point. This will likely lead to revolutionary changes. Tangible assets like real estate, art, and collectibles are where capital is moving because people want off the grid. By 2032, the Dow could reach 60,000, not because of economic strength but because of hyperinflation and a flight to tangible assets.

Host: What about cryptocurrencies?

Armstrong: Cryptocurrencies are being increasingly regulated. An organization above the United Nations, called FATF (Financial Action Task Force), is implementing know-your-customer rules and could force cryptos into a centralized IMF-backed digital currency. The IMF's goal is to replace the U.S. dollar as the world's reserve currency.

Host: And gold?

Armstrong: Gold has also been targeted by regulators. Twenty years ago, you could carry gold coins on a plane. Now, they're tracking every ounce. This isn't about conspiracy theories—it's about control.

Host: How do Russia and China fit into this?

Armstrong: Russia and China won't surrender their sovereignty to a one-world government. Schwab's vision of global governance cannot succeed without them. Historically, every attempt at global domination has failed, whether it was Napoleon, Hitler, or others.

Host: What about New York's decline?

Armstrong: New York is falling apart due to policies like eviction moratoriums. If landlords can't collect rent, they default on their mortgages, leading to foreclosures. It's a cascade of failure that could turn cities into ghettos. Miami is emerging as the financial capital of the U.S., while New York fades away.

Host: And climate change?

Armstrong: The UN is using the climate change narrative to justify global governance. They've proposed a 10% global tax under the Paris Accord. It's the same idea that created the EU—one government to prevent war. But human nature doesn't change, and regional differences will always lead to divisions.

Key Takeaways:

1. **The Great Reset:** A push for a one-world government threatens democracy and sovereignty, with Europe's financial collapse paving the way for centralized control.
2. **MMT's Risks:** Modern Monetary Theory has emboldened reckless spending, ignoring the historical consequences of unchecked money printing.
3. **Tangible Assets Thrive:** Amid economic uncertainty, tangible assets like real estate, art, and collectibles are becoming safe havens.
4. **Crypto Regulation:** Cryptocurrencies face increased regulation, and central authorities aim to co-opt them into IMF-backed digital currencies.
5. **Decline of Major Cities:** Policies like eviction moratoriums are accelerating the decline of cities like New York, while places like Miami rise as new financial hubs.

Final Thought:

As the world grapples with competing ideologies, economic turmoil, and shifting power dynamics, understanding historical cycles is crucial.

The move toward centralized governance and unrestricted money printing poses significant risks, but tangible assets and individual sovereignty offer pathways to navigate the uncertainty.

PANDEMIC, INFLATION, AND GLOBAL REALIGNMENTS (FEBRUARY 22, 2022)

Interview Summary:

In this thought-provoking discussion on *The Financial Survival Network*, host Kerry Lutz and Martin Armstrong of Armstrong Economics delve into the aftermath of pandemic policies, the rising specter of inflation, geopolitical tensions, and the erosion of confidence in governments worldwide. This wide-ranging conversation tackles everything from monetary policy failures to global governance trends and the potential for war in Ukraine.

Kerry Lutz: Welcome to *The Financial Survival Network*. It's February 22, 2022, and we're here with Martin Armstrong. Martin, always great to have you. Let's start with the big story—pandemic restrictions are lifting in many countries. Is this a net positive for the economy, or have we gone too far down the rabbit hole for it to matter?

Martin Armstrong: Thanks, Kerry. It depends on the country. In Europe, I'd say we're way too far down the rabbit hole. Their economic problems go far beyond the pandemic. Negative interest rates, introduced in 2014, have destroyed their bond market and revealed the failure of Keynesian economics.

In contrast, states like Florida lifted restrictions early and have fared better. But globally, the damage is done. The pandemic was a convenient scapegoat for deeper economic mismanagement, particularly in Europe.

Kerry Lutz: What's the core issue in Europe?

Martin Armstrong: Europe's problems stem from negative interest rates and fiscal mismanagement. Keynesian policies—lowering rates, increasing money supply—have failed to stimulate growth or inflation as intended. Instead, they've destabilized markets.

The repo crisis of 2019 highlighted this when U.S. banks refused to accept European sovereign debt as collateral. New York banks won't even value it at 10 cents on the dollar. This lack of trust underscores the systemic failure in Europe's financial system.

The so-called "Great Reset," championed by Klaus Schwab, is a ploy to cover these failures. The idea of owning nothing and being happy isn't about helping people—it's about masking defaults and preventing public uprisings over pension collapses.

Kerry Lutz: Inflation is hitting hard. Shadow Stats suggests it's as high as 14-15%. Can the Federal Reserve bring it down, or are we too far gone?

Martin Armstrong: Inflation is here to stay for now, driven more by supply chain disruptions than monetary policy. The pandemic restrictions decimated global logistics, and the effects are still rippling through the system.

The Fed is in a tight spot. Raising interest rates might help domestically, but it will worsen the debt crisis in emerging markets where dollar-denominated loans dominate. This echoes past crises, like the Swiss loan fiasco in the 1980s, where currency mismatches wiped out borrowers.

Kerry Lutz: Let's talk about confidence. How does that play into inflation and economic trends?

Martin Armstrong: Confidence is critical. Inflation spikes when people lose trust in the government and expect future prices to rise. This dynamic is unfolding now, exacerbated by poor governance and COVID mismanagement.

Look at historical examples like the Weimar Republic. Hyperinflation wasn't just about money printing—it was about a collapse in trust. People moved their wealth into tangible assets, from gold to real estate, to escape a failing system.

Kerry Lutz: Are precious metals the answer for today's environment?

Martin Armstrong: They're part of it. Precious metals hold value in times of uncertainty, but so do other tangible assets like real estate and equities. Capital is fleeing Europe and pouring into U.S. stocks and property, particularly in states like Florida. This isn't about speculative bubbles—it's about preserving wealth in the face of government failures.

Kerry Lutz: Shifting gears to China, their real estate market looks like it's following the U.S.'s 2008 path. Is there a way out for them?

Martin Armstrong: China faces a unique challenge. Many of its local governments and developers borrowed in dollars to take advantage of lower interest rates. As the dollar strengthens, these debts become unmanageable.

The Fed raising rates will amplify this crisis. China even urged the Fed not to raise rates, fearing the ripple effects on their economy and emerging markets. This dollar debt issue makes their housing crisis worse and limits their policy options.

Kerry Lutz: Let's talk geopolitics. Is the U.S. looking to Ukraine as a diversion from domestic issues?

Martin Armstrong: Absolutely. The Biden administration is in trouble domestically, with record-low confidence. They need a distraction, and Ukraine could serve that purpose.

The situation in Ukraine is complex. Eastern Ukraine is predominantly Russian-speaking and culturally aligned with Russia. Realistically, splitting the country along these lines would make sense, but geopolitics isn't about practicality. The U.S. seems intent on escalating tensions to shift focus away from COVID missteps.

Kerry Lutz: Schwab's "Great Reset" vision—where does it stand?

Martin Armstrong: Schwab has an iron grip on Europe, with key leaders like Ursula von der Leyen (EU), Christine Lagarde (ECB), and others aligned with his agenda. He envisions a Marxist-style utopia, but this vision is outdated.

In the 19th century, Marxism made some sense because most people owned nothing. Today, people have homes, cars, and savings. Schwab's idea of owning nothing doesn't resonate—it's detached from modern reality.

Kerry Lutz: What's your outlook for markets and global stability?

Martin Armstrong: Markets will likely soften in the short term but continue to rise as capital flows into U.S. equities from overseas. The Dow could reach 65,000 in the coming years as confidence in government collapses globally.

War is a real possibility, driven by political desperation. Governments may use conflict to distract from their failures and justify further control. The erosion of trust in institutions is accelerating, and this is the underlying driver of many trends we're seeing.

Kerry Lutz: As always, Martin, your insights are invaluable. Thanks for joining us.

Martin Armstrong: My pleasure, Kerry.

Key Takeaways:

1. **Europe's Economic Woes:** Negative rates and fiscal mismanagement have devastated confidence.

2. **Inflation:** A product of supply chain failures and collapsing trust, not just monetary policy.
3. **U.S. Markets:** Capital inflows from unstable regions will continue driving stocks and real estate.
4. **China's Dollar Debt Crisis:** Rising U.S. rates will exacerbate their housing and economic challenges.
5. **Geopolitics:** Ukraine could serve as a diversion for struggling governments like the U.S.

Final Thought

This conversation underscores the interconnectedness of global economic and political systems, emphasizing the need for vigilance in navigating these turbulent times.

THE END OF AN ERA? THE DOLLAR, GLOBAL INSTABILITY, AND THE PATH TO CONFLICT (JULY 19, 2022)

Interview Summary:

In this revealing interview, Martin Armstrong discusses the fragility of the global economic system, highlighting the weaponization of the U.S. dollar, the geopolitical implications of sanctions, and the erosion of trust in Western leadership. Armstrong examines commodity markets, China's real estate crisis, and Europe's energy dilemma, connecting these challenges to broader geopolitical tensions. He also critiques leadership failures and explores the potential for escalating war cycles, particularly in the context of the Ukraine conflict.

Kerry Lutz: Welcome back, Martin Armstrong. There's so much happening right now—oil price shocks, commodity swings, BRICS nations challenging the dollar, and what looks like Western civilization self-destructing. Let's start with the dollar. Can it retain its reserve currency status, and if so, for how long?

Martin Armstrong: The dollar's dominance comes from more than just commodities being priced in it. The key factor is its global accessibility. For example, if you want to issue a bond in yen, you need approval from Japan's Ministry of Finance. With dollars, you don't face such restrictions, making it the go-to currency for global transactions. Historically, we saw the same with British pounds pre-World War I. However, the U.S.'s weaponization of the dollar through sanctions, especially against Russia, has fundamentally shaken global confidence.

Kerry Lutz: How so?

Martin Armstrong: By targeting individual Russians and seizing assets without due process, the U.S. sent a dangerous message: If we don't like your country, we can come after your citizens. That undermines the global rule of law and the free movement of capital. Why would a Chinese investor risk putting money in the U.S. knowing their assets could be frozen arbitrarily?

Kerry Lutz: Is this the beginning of the end for the dollar as the world's reserve currency?

Martin Armstrong: It's heading that way. The split caused by these sanctions has pushed countries like China and Russia to seek alternatives. While the dollar won't disappear overnight, by 2024, this shift will become much more pronounced. Moves like removing Russia from SWIFT accelerated this process. Obama considered it in 2014 during the Crimea crisis but backed off, knowing it would destabilize the global financial system. Biden went ahead, showing either a lack of foresight or a deliberate push toward global destabilization.

Kerry Lutz: Could this be tied to a broader agenda, like the WEF's "Great Reset"?

Martin Armstrong: Klaus Schwab and his supporters are delusional. They think they can take down Russia and China without triggering a global conflict. That's insanity. Their policies are dismantling the West economically, driving us closer to chaos.

Kerry Lutz: Speaking of chaos, let's talk about the war in Ukraine. Was Russia provoked into this conflict?

Martin Armstrong: Absolutely. Just before Russia invaded, Zelensky openly talked about rearming Ukraine with nuclear weapons. That was a red line for Putin, especially given the agreements from 1994 guaranteeing Ukraine's neutrality. NATO expansion also violated prior treaties. This war was avoidable but deliberately escalated.

200

Kerry Lutz: What about commodities and energy prices?

Martin Armstrong: Energy will remain high, especially in Europe. The sanctions and mishandling of Russian energy supplies are catastrophic. For example, Germany delayed repairing turbines for gas pipelines under pressure from Ukraine. Now, Germany is facing an energy crisis so severe that they've issued guides on cooking without electricity. Europe's industrial heart is being gutted by its own policies.

Kerry Lutz: And China? Their real estate market seems to be in free fall.

Martin Armstrong: China's real estate bubble is massive, and the cracks are showing. Many provinces borrowed in dollars to save on interest, ignoring foreign exchange risks. As the dollar strengthens, their debt burden grows, similar to what happened in the 1980s with Swiss franc mortgages in Australia and Europe. This, combined with a slowing GDP, points to a major economic decline in China by 2023.

Kerry Lutz: What about gold and silver? They've been struggling.

Martin Armstrong: Gold's movements are tied to confidence in government, not inflation as many believe. The stronger dollar has pressured gold prices in dollar terms, but in other currencies, gold has held up better. Until confidence in government deteriorates further, gold won't see a major breakout.

Kerry Lutz: Finally, are we heading for a major war?

Martin Armstrong: The war cycle points to escalating conflict. NATO's reckless arming of Ukraine and its ammunition shortages suggest a lack of strategic foresight. Putin hasn't escalated to full-scale war—he's focused on protecting Russian-speaking regions like Donbass. This isn't about conquering Ukraine; it's about securing historical Russian territories.

Kerry Lutz: Sobering thoughts. Thanks, Martin. For more insights, visit ArmstrongEconomics.com and sign up for Martin's newsletter.

Martin Armstrong: Thank you, Kerry. Stay safe.

Key Takeaways:

1. The U.S. dollar's dominance is eroding due to its weaponization through sanctions, pushing countries toward alternatives like BRICS currencies.
2. Geopolitical tensions, particularly the Ukraine war, are exacerbating global economic instability, with NATO's actions escalating conflict.
3. Europe's energy crisis and China's real estate collapse highlight vulnerabilities in major economies.
4. Gold remains tied to confidence in government, while a strong dollar suppresses its dollar-denominated price.
5. The global war cycle suggests increasing conflict, with 2023 marking a potential turning point for geopolitical and economic chaos.

Final Thought:

As the dollar's dominance wanes and geopolitical tensions escalate, Armstrong warns of a turning point in global stability, with 2023 shaping up to be a year of unprecedented challenges.

Navigating Turbulence: Inflation, Unrest, and the Decline of Trust (Sept 22, 2022)

Interview Summary:

In this eye-opening conversation, Martin Armstrong outlines a survival roadmap for an increasingly unstable world. With political distrust, civil unrest, inflation, and global economic shifts on the rise, he warns of unprecedented challenges ahead. Armstrong shares insights into U.S. political polarization, the erosion of constitutional principles, the impact of inflation and shortages on global stability, and the escalating proxy war in Ukraine. Amid these crises, he offers pragmatic advice for personal preparedness and resilience.

Kerry Lutz: Martin Armstrong is back with us. If you haven't subscribed to his blog at ArmstrongEconomics.com, do it now. We're living in unprecedented times, and today we'll explore a roadmap for survival. Martin, welcome back. What should the average person be doing to navigate this chaos?

Martin Armstrong: Thanks, Kerry. It's tough. We're facing challenges on every front—politically, economically, and socially. I've been through my own battles, as you know. They kept me imprisoned for seven years under civil contempt, well beyond the 18-month statutory limit. The Supreme Court finally ordered my release. These experiences taught me that the Constitution means nothing to those in power unless they're forced to acknowledge it.

The same applies to what we're seeing now. Look at the recent raid on Trump's residence. This kind of targeting has turned the Justice Department into what I call the "Department of Just Us." It's all politically motivated, and my computer models are forecasting 2023 as a year of political hell.

Kerry Lutz: What does that mean?

Martin Armstrong: Neither side will accept the results of the November elections. We're likely to see massive civil unrest, something we haven't witnessed at this scale before. Biden won with a slim margin of about 51.3%, yet his administration acts as though it has an overwhelming mandate. This kind of governance isn't democratic— it's dictatorial.

Historically, even presidents who won with a real mandate, like Roosevelt or Johnson, governed more cautiously. Today, there's no such restraint. Combine that with policies that foster inflation and the green agenda's attack on fossil fuels, and you're left with an increasingly volatile society.

Kerry Lutz: Crime and social unrest are already palpable. Do you see this getting worse?

Martin Armstrong: Absolutely. Inflation, largely driven by lockdowns and supply chain disruptions, is making it worse. Farmers couldn't get their goods to market, leading to shortages. I had farmers emailing me—they had to kill thousands of chickens or let cattle starve. These disruptions are causing unrest worldwide, especially in countries like Sri Lanka and Lebanon, where rising energy costs are devastating.

Kerry Lutz: Is the unrest part of a larger design?

Martin Armstrong: I don't think it's a deliberate design—it's incompetence. Most policymakers are clueless. They see the world through their immediate surroundings and don't grasp global ripple effects. The inflationary spiral combined with attacks on fossil fuels is catastrophic. The zealots driving the green agenda think alternatives will magically appear, but that's not how markets work.

Kerry Lutz: What's your view on the 2022 elections?

Martin Armstrong: This election will be one of the most controversial in U.S. history. My models even show the possibility that the 2024 presidential election might not happen. Current political dynamics are unsustainable. Declaring war on half the population isn't governance—it's chaos.

Kerry Lutz: Let's talk about China. Their real estate market looks like a house of cards.

Martin Armstrong: China's problems stem from provinces and banks borrowing in dollars to save on interest. As the dollar strengthens, their debt burden becomes unsustainable. Combined with declining GDP and people fleeing cities like Shanghai, China faces stagflation—a combination of stagnation and inflation. The exodus from urban centers isn't just happening in China—it's global.

Kerry Lutz: And Europe?

Martin Armstrong: Europe's situation is dire, particularly Germany. Their energy crisis, fueled by the Ukraine conflict, is pushing them toward economic collapse. Germany is now telling citizens how to cook without electricity. If the winter is severe, many elderly people won't survive.

Kerry Lutz: What about the war in Ukraine?

Martin Armstrong: The Ukraine conflict is a proxy war against Russia, and it's spiraling out of control. The Donbass region has always been historically Russian. Continuing to fight over this territory is absurd, especially when agreements like Minsk promised self-determination. But this war isn't about Ukraine—it's about destabilizing Russia and maintaining control over energy routes.

Kerry Lutz: Let's shift to markets. Is the stock market poised to recover?

Martin Armstrong: Not immediately. We're looking at more declines through the elections and into January, which will be a difficult month. After that, geopolitical tensions, particularly in Ukraine, will drive capital flight to the U.S., as it did during World Wars I and II. This influx will likely boost U.S. blue-chip stocks and tangible assets like gold in the first quarter of 2023.

Kerry Lutz: What's your advice for individuals?

Martin Armstrong: Stock up on essentials. Food shortages are becoming more frequent, and agriculture is under strain. Have emergency supplies on hand—freezers, non-perishables, and basic necessities. This isn't about panic; it's about preparation.

Kerry Lutz: And what about the broader message for survival?

Martin Armstrong: Don't let fear control you. Governments thrive on creating fear to manipulate the population. Stay informed, stay rational, and focus on what you can control.

Kerry Lutz: Great advice, Martin. For more insights, visit ArmstrongEconomics.com. Thanks for joining us.

Martin Armstrong: Always a pleasure, Kerry. Take care.

Key Takeaways:

1. Civil unrest and political polarization are likely to escalate in 2023, fueled by distrust in governance and economic instability.
2. Inflation and supply chain disruptions, worsened by misguided policies, are driving global unrest and energy crises.
3. China's economic struggles and Europe's energy shortages highlight vulnerabilities in major economies, with global stagflation on the horizon.

4. Markets may recover in early 2023 as capital flows to the U.S. amid geopolitical chaos.
5. Preparation, not panic, is key: stock up on essentials and remain informed to navigate these turbulent times.

Final Thought:

As the world faces escalating unrest and uncertainty, Armstrong emphasizes the importance of preparation, resilience, and maintaining control of your own mind to weather the storm ahead.

THE RISE OF THE NEOCONS, UKRAINE, AND GLOBAL SHIFTS (MARCH 7, 2023)

Introductory Summary:

Martin Armstrong joins Kerry Lutz to discuss his latest book, *The Rise of the Neocons*, offering a deep dive into the Ukraine war, U.S. geopolitical strategy, and its implications for global stability. The conversation expands to include gold, central bank digital currencies (CBDCs), and the evolving economic order, with Armstrong presenting a sobering view of current leadership and systemic failures.

Kerry Lutz: Welcome to *The Financial Survival Network*. I'm your host, Kerry Lutz. It's March 7, 2023, and today we're thrilled to have Martin Armstrong back with us. Martin's new book, *The Rise of the Neocons*, is out now. We'll discuss it alongside the Ukraine war, gold, and central bank digital currencies. Martin, it's always a pleasure to have you. Let's start with Ukraine. What's really happening there, and when will it end?

Martin Armstrong: Thanks, Kerry. The Ukraine war could end in 15 minutes if both sides agreed to the Minsk Agreement.

Kerry Lutz: What's the Minsk Agreement?

Martin Armstrong: It was brokered after the 2014 revolution by Germany and France, with Putin's involvement. It allowed the Donbass region to vote for independence. The Donbass, historically Russian, was arbitrarily added to Ukraine by Khrushchev for administrative purposes during the Soviet era. When the Soviet Union collapsed,

Ukraine claimed the territory, but the population there is predominantly Russian.

The U.S. backed a 2014 revolution, installed an interim government, and immediately began attacking the Donbass. This has been a proxy war from the start, driven by figures like Victoria Nuland, who has deep ties to Ukraine. She was at Maidan during the revolution, handing out sandwiches. Her involvement illustrates how personal agendas often drive U.S. foreign policy.

Kerry Lutz: So this is essentially another endless war?

Martin Armstrong: Exactly. The neocons have been pushing wars for decades—Vietnam, Afghanistan, Iraq—and we've learned nothing. These conflicts have no strategic benefit for the U.S. All they achieve is more debt and more lives lost. The military-industrial complex, of course, profits immensely, but at what cost?

Kerry Lutz: The military-industrial complex must be thrilled with all the contracts.

Martin Armstrong: Yes, but even the U.S. military has told Biden they don't want boots on the ground in Ukraine. There's a divide between military leadership and political operatives like Zelensky, who refuses to retreat for fear of losing Western funding. Meanwhile, the Pandora Papers exposed Ukraine as the most corrupt country globally, with politicians—including Zelensky—stashing millions offshore.

Kerry Lutz: It's infuriating. And yet, people keep falling for it.

Martin Armstrong: Wars are driven by leaders, not the people. Hermann Göring said it best at the Nuremberg trials—leaders manipulate patriotism to drag people into war. The average citizen in Russia, China, or the U.S. just wants to work, support their family, and avoid conflict.

Kerry Lutz: What about China and Taiwan? Is an invasion imminent?

Martin Armstrong: Yes, it's likely. Public threats from the U.S. force China's hand—they can't appear weak. Pelosi's visit to Taiwan and congressional grandstanding are provocations. Diplomacy 101 teaches you to handle such matters behind closed doors. By escalating tensions publicly, the Biden administration has left China with little choice.

Kerry Lutz: Are we looking at global war soon?

Martin Armstrong: My models point to 2025–2027 as the period for a broader international war. If China takes Taiwan, North Korea invades the South, Russia takes Ukraine, and Iran attacks Israel and Saudi Arabia simultaneously, the U.S. doesn't have the resources to fight on multiple fronts.

Kerry Lutz: Turning to the economy, what's your outlook for the stock market?

Martin Armstrong: The market will eventually break to the upside. As governments face rising debt and default risks, capital will flow out of bonds and into private assets like stocks, gold, and real estate. This shift has already begun.

Kerry Lutz: Real estate in Florida is still booming. Why?

Martin Armstrong: Migration from high-tax states is driving demand. Many buyers here pay cash for homes, especially in the $1–5 million range. Florida's lack of income tax and better governance make it attractive. States like California, New York, and Illinois are hemorrhaging residents, and their fiscal policies are unsustainable.

Kerry Lutz: Let's talk gold. When will we see significant appreciation?

Martin Armstrong: Gold rises with declining confidence in government, not inflation. During geopolitical crises or when sovereign debt risks escalate, gold becomes a safe haven. With Europe's financial system crumbling—thanks to negative rates from 2014 –2022—gold will gain traction as people seek tangible assets.

Kerry Lutz: What about central bank digital currencies (CBDCs)?

Martin Armstrong: CBDCs are part of a broader plan to reset the financial system. After World War II, Bretton Woods restructured global finance. The elites envision something similar now, using CBDCs to manage debt defaults and control populations. Schwab's rhetoric about "owning nothing and being happy" is propaganda to sell this narrative.

Kerry Lutz: It's terrifying. Final thoughts, Martin?

Martin Armstrong: The key is awareness. Governments and elites are working behind the scenes to reshape the financial system. The public must understand that tangible assets—gold, real estate, and even certain stocks—will be crucial as the sovereign debt crisis unfolds.

Kerry Lutz: Well said. Martin's new book, *The Rise of the Neocons*, is a must-read. Visit ArmstrongEconomics.com for more insights. Thanks for joining us, Martin.

Martin Armstrong: Always a pleasure, Kerry. Take care.

Key Takeaways:

1. The Ukraine war and potential conflicts with China and Russia are driven by poor diplomacy and neoconservative agendas, not national interest.
2. Rising distrust in governments will lead to capital flows into tangible assets like gold, stocks, and real estate.
3. CBDCs may signal a financial system reset, with significant implications for individual freedom and financial stability.

Final Thought:

Armstrong emphasizes the need for vigilance and preparation as geopolitical tensions, economic instability, and government overreach reshape the global landscape.

DE-DOLLARIZATION AND GLOBAL TURBULENCE: NAVIGATING ECONOMIC SHIFTS (AUGUST 3, 2023)

Interview Summary:

In this in-depth discussion, Martin Armstrong addresses the global movement toward de-dollarization, the fragmentation of international finance, and the emerging economic challenges driven by geopolitical conflict. Exploring the implications of sanctions, banking instability, and shifting capital flows, Armstrong critiques the policies fueling these crises. He also offers insights on market behavior, the persistence of inflation, and the critical role of resilience in navigating these volatile times.

Kerry Lutz: Welcome back to *The Financial Survival Network*. It's August 3, 2023, and we're thrilled to have Martin Armstrong here. Martin, your upcoming book, *De-Dollarization*, is highly anticipated. Let's start with the dollar's recent fluctuations. Is de-dollarization fact or fiction?

Martin Armstrong: Thanks, Kerry. *De-Dollarization* is partially fact, but it's also a reaction to geopolitical events. The U.S. dollar remains dominant due to the depth of its financial markets, just like Britain's pound sterling before World War I. Countries issue bonds in dollars because it's the most liquid and trusted currency.

However, the Biden administration's decision to weaponize the SWIFT system by excluding Russia sent a strong signal to the world: the U.S. can cut you off if it disapproves of your actions. This has led to the fragmentation of global finance, with China and Iran setting up alternatives. It's not about deficits or debt levels—it's a geopolitical shift.

Kerry Lutz: If de-dollarization gains momentum, what's the alternative? A BRICS currency?

Martin Armstrong: A BRICS currency sounds appealing on paper, but it's unrealistic. None of these countries have financial systems capable of supporting global trade or investment at the scale of the U.S. Instead, they're responding to threats by reducing reliance on the dollar. China, for example, has been selling U.S. debt every month. You can't blame them—they're not going to fund a government that might use those resources against them.

Kerry Lutz: How does this affect interest rates?

Martin Armstrong: As foreign buyers reduce their purchases of U.S. debt, interest rates must rise to attract investors. The Federal Reserve can't control this dynamic—it's out of their hands now. Geopolitics has taken over, and that's what's driving rates up.

Kerry Lutz: What about the banking sector? Are we looking at another crisis like 2008-2009?

Martin Armstrong: The situation is worse in Europe than in the U.S. Europe's negative interest rates since 2014 created significant losses for banks and pension funds. Now, rising rates are forcing them to reprice their bond portfolios, eroding capital further. In the U.S., failures like SVB reveal a lack of expertise on bank boards. Many decisions are driven by political agendas rather than financial merit.

Kerry Lutz: How far can the Fed push rates before it breaks something?

Martin Armstrong: Powell has no choice but to keep raising rates. With China and others stepping back from buying U.S. debt, rates must rise to find buyers. It's not just about inflation anymore—it's a structural shift in the global financial system.

Kerry Lutz: Despite this, the stock market seems resilient. Why?

Martin Armstrong: Historically, rising interest rates don't always crash the market. In fact, they signal demand for money. Investors are diversifying into tangible assets—real estate, gold, and even stocks. Bonds, the traditional safe haven, aren't as attractive in this environment.

Kerry Lutz: Speaking of real estate, Florida's market remains strong. Will it stay that way?

Martin Armstrong: Yes, for now. The migration from northern states to places like Florida is driving demand. Many buyers are paying cash, especially for homes in the $1–5 million range, which insulates the market from higher mortgage rates.

Kerry Lutz: Can states like New York and California survive these population shifts?

Martin Armstrong: Not without significant restructuring. These states rely heavily on high-income earners who are leaving in droves. Their fiscal policies are unsustainable, and bailouts from the federal government won't fix the underlying issues.

Kerry Lutz: Let's talk about AI. How do you see it shaping the future?

Martin Armstrong: AI has incredible potential, but it depends on how it's applied. For example, we've used AI since the 1970s to analyze financial markets. However, fears about AI taking over are exaggerated—it's only as good as the data and objectives it's given. The real danger is using AI irresponsibly, such as in autonomous weapons.

Kerry Lutz: On that note, the Ukraine conflict shows the darker side of technological advancements, like drone warfare. What's your take?

Martin Armstrong: The Ukraine war highlights how technology can escalate conflicts. It's not just about geopolitics—it's about maintaining the military-industrial complex. Weapons are destroyed, creating demand for replacements. This cycle of destruction and rearmament fuels the economy for a select few, but at a massive human cost.

Kerry Lutz: Final thoughts, Martin?

Martin Armstrong: Prepare for more instability. Stock up on essentials and tangible assets. Governments are spending recklessly, and central banks can't fix structural problems with rate hikes. As always, stay informed and focus on what you can control.

Kerry Lutz: Wise advice, as always. Martin's new book, *De-Dollarization*, will be out soon. Visit ArmstrongEconomics.com for updates. Thanks for joining us, Martin.

Martin Armstrong: Always a pleasure, Kerry. Take care.

Key Takeaways:

1. The push for de-dollarization is driven by geopolitics, not economic fundamentals. Alternatives like a BRICS currency lack the financial infrastructure to replace the dollar.
2. Rising interest rates are now a structural necessity as foreign buyers step back from U.S. debt.
3. The banking sector faces challenges from past low-rate policies and insufficient expertise on boards.
4. Tangible assets like real estate, gold, and stocks are gaining favor as traditional safe havens lose appeal.

5. Global instability will persist, requiring individuals to focus on preparedness and resilience.

Final Thought:

In an era of geopolitical fragmentation and economic uncertainty, Armstrong urges individuals to adapt by diversifying into tangible assets and prioritizing preparedness to navigate the challenges ahead.

CYCLES OF CONFLICT, TECHNOLOGY, AND CONTROL: THE WORLD ACCORDING TO MARTIN ARMSTRONG (OCTOBER 19, 2023)

Interview Summary:

In installment five of *The World According to Martin Armstrong*, Martin Armstrong and Kerry Lutz delve into the persistence of endless wars, the inefficiency of communism, the evolving influence of AI, and the rise of surveillance states. The discussion reflects on historical cycles, the role of technology in shaping economies, and the challenges of maintaining individual freedoms in an increasingly controlled global landscape.

Kerry Lutz: Welcome to *The Financial Survival Network*. I'm your host, Kerry Lutz. Today, we bring you installment five of *The World According to Martin Armstrong*. Marty, as always, thanks for joining us. The world seems consumed by endless wars. What's your take on the current conflicts?

Martin Armstrong: Thanks, Kerry. When you look at wars like those in Ukraine or the Middle East, you have to ask: what's the end goal? Does Ukraine seriously think it can destroy Russia? Or does Hamas believe it can eradicate Israel? These ideas are absurd. But peace is impossible if no one is willing to talk.

Kerry Lutz: It feels like the military-industrial complex and neocons thrive on perpetual conflict.

Martin Armstrong: Absolutely. Some of these people regret that the Cold War ended without a full-blown fight. Communism collapsed under its inefficiency, not military pressure. But instead of recognizing that, they continue to push for war.

Kerry Lutz: Speaking of inefficiency, you've often said communism fails because it denies the price mechanism.

Martin Armstrong: Exactly. When I visited China in the late 1990s after the Asian currency crisis, they were curious about capitalism. They monitored everything, including why tea sold for different prices in different places. I explained transportation costs, and they were shocked by the simplicity. Communism collapses because it stifles innovation and denies basic economic principles.

Kerry Lutz: China now faces its own inefficiencies—real estate implosions and crumbling infrastructure.

Martin Armstrong: They're learning, but it takes time. At least they understand the need for a consumer-based economy, unlike Germany, which relies heavily on exports. China's trying to shift its model, but it's not there yet.

Kerry Lutz: Back to wars—why do we see this constant push for escalation?

Martin Armstrong: Escalation is driven by arrogance and bad strategy. Giving Ukraine long-range missiles to attack Russia isn't about defense; it's about provocation. Similarly, Israel and Hamas are trapped in cycles of retaliation. Without dialogue, these conflicts can't end.

Kerry Lutz: Let's pivot to the economy. What's happening with the U.S. dollar and the BRICS currency?

Martin Armstrong: The dollar isn't going anywhere soon. Its strength comes from being the backbone of global finance. Emerging markets borrow in dollars because the U.S. has the world's deepest financial markets. BRICS currencies can't compete with that.

Kerry Lutz: What about the push for central bank digital currencies (CBDCs)?

Martin Armstrong: CBDCs are about control. Governments estimate they could collect 35% more in taxes by eliminating cash. They'll frame it as progress, but it's really about surveillance and revenue.

Kerry Lutz: Speaking of control, let's talk about Elon Musk. What's your view of his influence on media and technology?

Martin Armstrong: Musk has exposed government manipulation of social media, which is critical. Governments are becoming desperate as their systems falter. Musk's ventures like SpaceX and AI are reshaping industries, but AI isn't the existential threat people fear. It's a tool, not a sentient being.

Kerry Lutz: AI will eliminate some jobs, though.

Martin Armstrong: Yes, but technological change always does. Schumpeter called it "creative destruction." Cars replaced horse-drawn carriages. AI will replace certain roles, but it won't replace human imagination or curiosity—traits that drive real innovation.

Kerry Lutz: Final thoughts, Martin?

Martin Armstrong: The cycles of history—conflict, innovation, and societal change—are unstoppable. The key is understanding them and adapting. Governments may try to control everything, but innovation and individual resilience often prevail.

Kerry Lutz: As always, fascinating insights. Visit ArmstrongEconomics.com for more. Thanks, Martin, and we'll see you next time.

Martin Armstrong: Thank you, Kerry.

Key Takeaways:

1. Endless wars persist due to ideological rigidity and lack of dialogue.
2. Communism and centrally planned systems fail due to inefficiency and lack of innovation.
3. The dollar remains dominant, while CBDCs pose significant risks to individual freedoms.
4. Technological progress, including AI, drives economic shifts but doesn't threaten human creativity.

Final Thought:

Martin Armstrong highlights the enduring relevance of historical cycles, the perils of centralized control, and the transformative potential of technology in shaping the future.

THE ELECTION, ECONOMIC STAGFLATION, AND ESCALATING WAR RISK (JANUARY 29, 2024)

Interview Summary:

In this discussion on *The Financial Survival Network*, Martin Armstrong joins Kerry Lutz to analyze the current state of U.S. elections, markets, and global economic pressures. Armstrong's Socrates model has projected a potential landslide win for Trump in 2024, showing a significant voter swing toward anti-establishment candidates due to diminishing confidence in the government. Armstrong discusses the unique challenges facing traditional institutions, including mounting public debt, intensifying social divides, and signs of declining faith in both American and European governance.

The conversation highlights an impending economic downturn with stagflation and war concerns. Armstrong warns that inflation pressures and supply chain disruptions, exacerbated by political decisions, could continue into the decade. Global inflation, like that in the 1970s, persists amid stagnant growth, with confidence in government bonds plummeting. The result is increased interest in gold and private investments. Armstrong also foresees potential geopolitical manipulation, with U.S. leaders possibly igniting a conflict to divert attention from domestic troubles and bolster re-election chances. The conversation closes with Armstrong's outlook on structural shifts in global finance, from the U.S. dollar's weakening dominance to potential decentralized economic models, as nations explore alternatives to Western-controlled financial systems.

Kerry Lutz: Welcome back, Martin! Always great to have you. There's a lot to unpack—the election forecast, economic turbulence, and the global outlook. What are you seeing for the 2024 election?

Martin Armstrong: Thanks, Kerry. Our model, Socrates, has been highly accurate in political forecasting since 1985. For 2024, it's showing a dramatic lead for Trump, around 61%, which is remarkable. Typically, U.S. elections are much closer, with winners like Obama barely hitting 51%. This time, though, the model shows a significant shift, likely reflecting how deeply people distrust the establishment.

Kerry Lutz: It sounds like people are just fed up. Are you seeing this elsewhere?

Martin Armstrong: Absolutely. We're seeing this trend globally. In Europe, confidence in government is down to 30%, and there's rising support for parties outside the mainstream, like Germany's AFD. It's driven by policies that many feel have gone too far, like extreme climate change agendas and Central Bank Digital Currencies (CBDCs). Trump, by contrast, is against CBDCs, war, and radical climate initiatives—all issues resonating with frustrated voters.

Kerry Lutz: And with these large margins, it's almost too big for any tampering to change, right?

Martin Armstrong: That's right. It's hard to manipulate numbers this large. But we're also seeing some troubling rhetoric, like recent calls from prominent figures hinting that drastic measures may be needed to stop Trump. When someone puts out images of bullet holes and implications about removing Trump, you wonder how far they'll go to prevent him from winning.

Kerry Lutz: Turning to the economy, what are you forecasting for the markets this year?

Martin Armstrong: January was a critical month, marking a major turning point. We'll likely see a high followed by a back-off, maybe

226

until May. But longer-term, the lack of confidence in government bonds could drive people into the stock market. This isn't 1929. Today, we have a global debt crisis, which makes government bonds less attractive. People are more likely to keep assets in private markets than buy government debt.

Kerry Lutz: You've also talked about stagflation—similar to the 1970s—where we have inflation without growth. What's behind this?

Martin Armstrong: Yes, we're seeing stagflation because of supply-side disruptions from COVID, not speculative demand. As global tensions increase, we'll continue to have shortages, which leads to inflation, but without the corresponding economic growth. This economic strain will persist into the next few years, similar to the stagflationary period during the OPEC crisis.

Kerry Lutz: With inflation and a possible recession, what are your thoughts on alternative investments?

Martin Armstrong: Gold remains a strong hedge. When government bonds look risky, people turn to tangible assets like gold. And with global instability, more capital flows into the U.S. as a safe haven, which could keep stock prices buoyant. Yet, this trend will face pressure if war breaks out or if confidence in the U.S. government collapses.

Kerry Lutz: You mentioned war concerns. Could the U.S. actually start a war to divert attention from domestic issues?

Martin Armstrong: It's possible. History shows that no president has lost re-election during a war. There are rumors of a possible conflict this summer as a way to boost Biden's chances or to tie Trump's hands if he wins. Many believe they'll use war as a means of political diversion since the debt crisis makes funding social programs increasingly challenging.

Kerry Lutz: Speaking of debt, the U.S. is at a tipping point with a trillion-dollar interest expense. How sustainable is this?

Martin Armstrong: It's unsustainable. The debt is skyrocketing, and China, the largest holder of U.S. debt, is becoming increasingly wary of buying more. Once foreign buyers pull out, it becomes nearly impossible to issue new debt to pay off the old. This is how governments collapse—they can't pay their debts, and they start defaulting. I believe we're getting close to that scenario.

Kerry Lutz: And what about the dollar's future as a global reserve currency?

Martin Armstrong: The dollar will remain important, but it won't be the exclusive reserve currency. Sanctions on Russia pushed many countries to seek alternatives, and the IMF is pushing a digital coin to replace the dollar. The dollar's future depends on the U.S. economy remaining a major player. But with these sanctions, we're dividing the global economy and creating incentives for countries to shift away from the dollar.

Kerry Lutz: With all this chaos, how do we prepare?

Martin Armstrong: Focus on tangible assets and stay away from long-term government bonds. The next few years will bring uncertainty, especially with rising inflation and political instability. Remember, this isn't about partisan views. It's about understanding what's coming based on economic realities and adjusting accordingly.

Kerry Lutz: Thank you, Martin. For those listening, you can find more insights at ArmstrongEconomics.com. It's crucial to stay informed and prepared.

Martin Armstrong: Thanks, Kerry. Stay informed and take care.

Key Takeaways:

1. **Election Forecast:** Socrates predicts a landslide Trump victory, reflecting growing distrust in government and establishment parties worldwide.
2. **Stagflation Concerns:** Economic conditions mirror the 1970s, with inflation persisting amid stagnant growth due to supply chain disruptions and geopolitical tensions.
3. **Gold as a Safe Haven:** Gold continues to attract interest as a hedge against economic instability and geopolitical risk. Physical holdings are preferable over government bonds.
4. **Debt and Default Risks:** Rising U.S. debt levels, coupled with foreign buyers pulling out, signal a looming fiscal crisis that could trigger defaults.
5. **Dollar's Role in Transition:** The dollar remains dominant but faces growing competition from alternatives driven by sanctions and international distrust of U.S. policies.

Final Thought:

As political and economic instability grows, understanding trends and preparing with tangible investments is crucial. The next few years will demand foresight, adaptability, and careful financial planning to navigate the challenges ahead.

POLITICAL UPHEAVAL, FINANCIAL MARKETS, AND THE TREND TOWARD GLOBAL STAGFLATION (JUNE 21, 2024)

Interview Summary:

In this candid discussion on *The Financial Survival Network*, Martin Armstrong and host Kerry Lutz explore the upcoming U.S. election, the potential economic implications, and the concerning trend toward global stagflation. Armstrong argues that Trump's experience in Washington has armed him with insights into the "game" played by the establishment, and if re-elected, he intends to place his own trusted allies in key positions. However, resistance from entrenched political elites, whom Armstrong suspects may attempt to sideline Trump by any means, remains high. Armstrong warns of a prolonged recessionary period through 2028, citing COVID-induced supply chain disruptions and rising geopolitical tensions as triggers for global stagflation. He compares current conditions to the 1970s, when stagflation gripped economies due to energy price spikes and slow economic growth. In a politically polarized world, Armstrong notes, traditional fiscal and economic policy approaches may prove ineffective, leaving citizens, markets, and governments navigating uncharted waters. He underscores the value of gold as a hedge and sees the dollar's dominance challenged by geopolitical shifts and distrust of U.S. policy.

Kerry Lutz: Welcome back, Martin! So much going on—this election, the economy, and the global outlook. What's the latest from Socrates? Has anything shifted?

Martin Armstrong: Thanks, Kerry. No, Socrates still shows Trump winning, and it's not just a close call. This trend we're seeing isn't limited to the U.S.; it's global. Look at Europe's recent elections. We're seeing a major swing away from the establishment, and, ironically, today's so-called "far-right" parties are the ones opposing war while the centrists push for it.

Kerry Lutz: We're witnessing political lines getting blurred. So, what are the elites so worried about with Trump?

Martin Armstrong: They worry because he understands the game now. When he first took office, he let the establishment pick his cabinet, and they filled it with people like John Bolton, who undermined him. If he wins this time, he's made it clear that he'll bring his own people, which terrifies them. These elites have been working for decades, and they see Trump as the anti-war candidate, a threat to their power.

Kerry Lutz: And there's talk of dirty tricks, even a possible false flag, to prevent him from winning. Do you think they'd go that far?

Martin Armstrong: They might. They're very close to their goals and don't want to lose power. His anti-war stance puts him at odds with people like Victoria Nuland and others in D.C. who have spent their entire lives focused on "containing" Russia. The establishment could resort to extreme measures if they think they're at risk of losing everything.

Kerry Lutz: And what about the economic outlook? We've seen gold and silver reaching new highs. Is this a trend that will continue?

Martin Armstrong: Absolutely. We've entered a period of stagflation similar to the 1970s. This time, though, it was COVID that disrupted supply chains and caused inflation from shortages. People are feeling uncertain about the future, which affects consumer spending and creates a recessionary environment. I expect this downturn to last into

2028, with stagflation hanging around as inflation persists despite low growth.

Kerry Lutz: So with a recession through 2028, what does that mean for markets and inflation?

Martin Armstrong: We'll see stagflation—rising costs of production with minimal economic growth. COVID-induced supply shortages caused the initial inflation, and geopolitical tensions are making it worse. People are holding back on spending, which will continue until the uncertainty clears, probably sometime next year. But the longer-term trend points to a weaker economy, with inflation persisting in areas like energy and essential goods.

Kerry Lutz: It sounds like the environment is hostile for investors. How does this impact stock markets and bond yields?

Martin Armstrong: Markets will pull back initially due to recession fears and war uncertainty, but they'll eventually rally as people realize bonds aren't safe. Why would anyone want to sell stocks to buy government bonds from a spend-happy administration? The stock market may see some turbulence, but over the long haul, it'll rise as bonds increasingly look riskier due to massive government spending and looming defaults.

Kerry Lutz: And what about the dollar? Is there a global movement to move away from it?

Martin Armstrong: Yes, the dollar's dominance is being questioned because the U.S. used it as a weapon, especially with sanctions. This has driven nations toward alternatives like BRICS, not because of fiat currency issues but as a reaction to the dollar's politicization. Now, we're seeing shifts toward alternatives for international transactions. The IMF has even proposed a digital coin to replace the dollar in global reserves.

Kerry Lutz: Wow, those are some big shifts. So, bottom line: should investors be thinking about gold or other safe havens?

Martin Armstrong: Absolutely. Gold will remain a hedge, especially as trust in government bonds declines. We'll see stock markets fluctuate, but they'll stabilize and rise once it's clear that bonds are vulnerable. Investors need to understand that government policies are increasingly out of control, especially as they lean into war spending. Gold, as well as tangible assets, will offer stability in these uncertain times.

Kerry Lutz: Thank you, Martin. This has been incredibly insightful. For anyone listening, head over to ArmstrongEconomics.com for Martin's latest updates.

Martin Armstrong: Thank you, Kerry. We're living in unprecedented times, and it's crucial to stay informed and prepared.

Key Takeaways:

1. **Global Political Shifts:** The trend against establishment parties is intensifying globally, with significant implications for U.S. elections and foreign policy.
2. **Stagflation Threat:** The economy faces prolonged stagflation driven by COVID-related disruptions and geopolitical tensions, likely persisting through 2028.
3. **Gold as a Hedge:** Gold continues to be a preferred hedge against government instability and geopolitical risks, with physical holdings recommended over digital assets or government bonds.
4. **Dollar Dominance Questioned:** The weaponization of the dollar through sanctions has spurred global moves toward alternative financial systems, including BRICS and potential IMF digital currencies.

5. **Market Volatility and Opportunity:** While markets may face turbulence, stocks are expected to recover as bonds lose appeal due to excessive government spending and rising risks of default.

Final Thought:

As political and economic tensions escalate, safeguarding wealth through tangible assets like gold and adapting investment strategies to the evolving global landscape are critical. The coming years will demand vigilance, resilience, and a deep understanding of historical and current cycles to navigate effectively.

POWER, CRISES, AND FINANCIAL STRATEGIES IN A TUMULTUOUS ELECTION YEAR (JULY 26, 2024)

Interview Summary:

In this session with Martin Armstrong and host Kerry Lutz on *The Financial Survival Network*, Armstrong delves into political intrigue, global instability, and strategies for navigating the volatile economy of 2024. He highlights escalating political polarization, leadership challenges, and the potential for sudden shifts in candidates leading up to the U.S. presidential election. Armstrong's models predict a strong showing for Republicans, with a mandate reminiscent of Grover Cleveland's non-consecutive terms. He explores parallels between historical debt crises, like the defaults of ancient Greece, and current U.S. fiscal challenges, noting the economic risks of war and governmental overreach. Armstrong underscores the continued appeal of gold as a hedge against global uncertainty and advises caution with government bonds amid potential currency and market disruptions.

Kerry Lutz: Welcome back, Martin! Today we're looking at global instability, the election, and what all this means for the markets. There's a lot happening, and it feels like we're on the edge of a major change.

Martin Armstrong: Thanks, Kerry. Yes, history is repeating itself—political games, economic chaos, and distrust in leadership. Governments across the world are grappling with legitimacy issues. It's not just here in the U.S.; you see the same discontent in Europe, Canada, and beyond. The global confidence in government has collapsed.

Kerry Lutz: We're seeing polarization unlike anything in recent memory. And here, it seems like the election is being set up. What are your thoughts on what we're witnessing?

Martin Armstrong: This year has been particularly strategic. Biden's administration has kept the Democratic ticket narrow, aiming to control the timing and narrative of his potential exit. I wouldn't be surprised if we see an unexpected candidate step in at the last minute, keeping the Republicans guessing.

Kerry Lutz: And there's talk of a brokered convention, with figures like Hillary or even Michelle Obama as potential candidates. How does your computer model see the election playing out?

Martin Armstrong: Our model's been consistent, predicting a Republican win with a strong margin—around 59–61%. This is unusual; historically, most U.S. elections have been tight. The model doesn't focus on candidates themselves but on broader trends, showing a global shift against incumbents. That sentiment favors a Republican win, even without Trump.

Kerry Lutz: Given this, what do you think will happen in the markets? People are wondering if the political turmoil will lead to recession or even war.

Martin Armstrong: We're heading into stagflation similar to the 1970s. COVID-driven supply chain issues started the inflation we're seeing, and the sanctions on Russia have only worsened things. This spending is unsustainable, and we're likely facing a recession through 2028. We'll also see more global realignment, as nations move away from the dollar in response to U.S. foreign policy.

Kerry Lutz: Is this what's driving the interest in gold, then?

Martin Armstrong: Yes, the demand for gold is geopolitical. As countries like China move away from U.S. debt, they're buying gold as a neutral asset in case of conflict. This isn't about inflation; it's about hedging against geopolitical risk. My advice: prioritize physical precious metals over digital assets or government bonds. During a crisis, governments have historically restricted access to gold or financial markets.

Kerry Lutz: And on top of that, the drumbeat toward war seems constant. Is this all part of the cycle you often talk about?

Martin Armstrong: Unfortunately, yes. History shows that governments often turn to war to reset debt and political issues. We saw it after the Panic of 1837, and it looks similar today. Countries need an excuse to default on their debts, and war gives them a way out. People should be ready for more volatility, and I expect gold and silver to be safe-haven assets, especially if war becomes imminent.

Kerry Lutz: So you're predicting a market pullback by September, with war and recession as long-term threats?

Martin Armstrong: Correct. I expect a dip in the markets by September. This setup could be intensified by actions from politicians, both domestically and abroad, especially as they plan for a new administration. It's wise to hedge with gold, watch the markets carefully, and understand the risks tied to geopolitical instability.

Kerry Lutz: Thank you, Martin. This is valuable insight for navigating what feels like a historic crossroads. To everyone listening, head to ArmstrongEconomics.com for Martin's updates.

Martin Armstrong: Thank you, Kerry. It's more important than ever to stay informed and prepared for what's coming.

Key Takeaways:

1. **Political Shifts:** Biden's administration is keeping options open for unexpected Democratic candidates, while models predict a strong Republican win in 2024.
2. **Stagflation and Realignment:** Global economic trends point to stagflation, with countries moving away from U.S. financial systems due to policy and sanctions.
3. **Gold as a Geopolitical Hedge:** Gold demand is rising, driven by geopolitical risks rather than inflation concerns, with a focus on physical holdings over digital or paper assets.
4. **Cycles of War and Economic Disruption:** Historical patterns suggest governments often resort to war during financial crises to reset debts and distract from internal instability.
5. **Market Caution:** Expect a pullback in September and prepare for prolonged volatility through 2028 by diversifying assets and prioritizing safe havens like gold and silver.

Final Thought:

In a year of political and economic uncertainty, staying informed and diversifying investments in tangible assets like gold and silver can provide security amid global volatility. Understanding historical cycles and current trends is essential for navigating these tumultuous times.

Power Struggles, Economic Turmoil, and Global Tensions in 2024 (September 21, 2024)

Interview Summary:

Kerry Lutz and Martin Armstrong delve into the state of the U.S. government, international relations, and the economic outlook for 2024 and beyond. Armstrong expresses concern over the current administration's reliance on a bureaucratic "deep state" and speculates that figures like Biden and Harris are seen as easier to control by powerful, unelected officials. He warns of the risks posed by neoconservative foreign policy agendas, noting that these individuals have pushed the U.S. into conflicts since the Cold War, often under misleading pretenses. Armstrong is also wary of rising tensions with Russia, China, and other nations, highlighting the economic implications of de-dollarization and increasing international efforts to detach from U.S. financial systems.

Kerry Lutz: Welcome back, Martin. You know, we're living in strange times with government power plays, foreign policy crises, and economic instability. What's your take on what's happening right now?

Martin Armstrong: Thanks for having me, Kerry. Right now, we're witnessing a power struggle between entrenched interests and the American people. There's a deep state that wields power beyond the administration—unelected bureaucrats who've held sway for decades, regardless of the president.

Kerry Lutz: You're saying that figures like Biden and Harris are easy for them to manage?

Martin Armstrong: Exactly. The neocons want influence without a strong leader getting in their way. They're focused on exerting control, even if it means risking international conflicts. Their fixation on spreading democracy—or at least, on expanding influence—has led to almost every U.S. military engagement since World War II. And in recent years, this approach has reached new extremes.

Kerry Lutz: And you're concerned about the implications, especially with Russia and China?

Martin Armstrong: Absolutely. We've antagonized major powers. Removing Russia from the SWIFT system, for instance, was a wake-up call for many countries, prompting them to look for alternatives. BRICS nations are now exploring ways to sidestep the U.S. dollar, not out of financial strategy but for protection from potential sanctions.

Kerry Lutz: So is this "de-dollarization" going to weaken the U.S. economy?

Martin Armstrong: It could. We've forced other nations to consider other financial systems, including relying on gold. For them, gold is neutral and less vulnerable to sanctions. It's not about investment—it's about hedging against potential U.S. defaults if tensions escalate. We're also seeing China divest U.S. Treasury bonds. This isn't about the dollar going to zero, but it's changing global finance dynamics.

Kerry Lutz: What's your outlook for the economy in the next couple of years? Will we see a recession, stagflation, or worse?

Martin Armstrong: It's looking like stagflation. We're seeing inflation due to supply chain disruptions from COVID, rather than just monetary policy. My models show a downturn lasting until around 2028, much like the 1970s, with stagnant growth and inflation. The political instability and risk of global conflict are only going to heighten the uncertainty.

Kerry Lutz: What about gold and silver as safe-haven assets?

Martin Armstrong: Gold's current rise is largely driven by geopolitical concerns rather than inflation. It's about the risk of global conflicts and currency instability. With talk of potential wars, people are looking for security, so gold prices could go even higher. However, in times of conflict, there's a history of governments suspending gold markets or imposing capital controls, so physical gold might be safer than gold on paper.

Kerry Lutz: Are you suggesting that people focus on physical silver as well?

Martin Armstrong: Yes. Silver coins—particularly pre-1965—could be valuable in an underground economy if financial systems are disrupted. Silver may be more accessible than gold and could still hold substantial value. I'd advise holding physical precious metals over digital assets like Bitcoin, which can be tracked and potentially controlled.

Kerry Lutz: Do you think governments would try to shut down digital assets like Bitcoin in a time of crisis?

Martin Armstrong: They might. Bitcoin transactions are traceable, which governments find convenient. Many of us in the tech community believe Bitcoin was intended to track digital transactions. In a crisis, precious metals would likely be a more secure asset.

Kerry Lutz: This conversation has been fascinating, Martin. I'll make sure to share this with our audience and let them know to follow you at ArmstrongEconomics.com. Thank you for taking the time today.

Martin Armstrong: Thanks for having me, Kerry. It's important to understand what's happening in these turbulent times.

Key Takeaways:

1. **Deep State Dynamics:** Unelected bureaucrats and neoconservative policies continue to shape U.S. government actions and foreign policy, often leading to global tensions.
2. **De-Dollarization Trends:** Countries are actively exploring alternatives to the U.S. dollar, prompted by economic sanctions and geopolitical concerns.
3. **Stagflation Concerns:** Economic models predict stagnant growth and inflation similar to the 1970s, exacerbated by political instability and global conflict risks.
4. **Precious Metals as Security:** Physical gold and silver remain vital safe-haven assets, particularly in times of conflict and financial instability.
5. **Risks to Digital Assets:** Governments may target digital assets like Bitcoin during crises, increasing the importance of tangible investments.

Final Thought:

The economic and geopolitical landscape of 2024 is fraught with risks, from de-dollarization to stagflation and rising tensions with global powers. Understanding these trends and preparing with tangible assets can help navigate this uncertain future.

THE POST-ELECTION LANDSCAPE AND SHIFTING POWER DYNAMICS (NOVEMBER 11, 2024)

Interview Summary:

The 2024 election has ended with Trump winning decisively, and Kerry Lutz and Martin Armstrong reflect on the implications of this outcome. Armstrong, who had previously predicted Trump's victory based on economic trends, discusses the left's response, marked by disbelief and protests. He also analyzes how political infighting and criminal charges against Trump backfired, leading to a stronger position for him and the Republican platform. Armstrong highlights that Trump's return will likely bring immediate changes, including swift policy reversals in foreign and domestic agendas, particularly around immigration, economic reforms, and an emphasis on de-escalating overseas conflicts.

The conversation extends to the international stage, with Armstrong noting the shift in global sentiment against long-standing Western policies, particularly NATO's role in global conflicts. Armstrong predicts that neoconservatives may attempt to counter Trump's agenda, especially his desire to end U.S. involvement in international wars. He foresees challenges in reining in national debt and suggests a shift toward tariffs and less borrowing. Armstrong emphasizes the potential for a major economic reset as the public turns away from "socialist" and "neo-Marxist" influences, with the decline of these ideologies expected to complete around 2037.

Kerry Lutz: The election's over, and Martin Armstrong is here with us. He's been predicting Trump's win for nearly a year, with his models showing a high probability. Martin, great to have you on! With the election done, what do you see happening next?

Martin Armstrong: Great to be back, Kerry. This outcome didn't surprise me; the economics predicted it. There was a strong likelihood people would turn away from the current administration because of the economic challenges. The left is in shock—they assumed criminal charges and the media focus on Trump would make him unelectable, but it backfired. They underestimated the public's focus on economic realities.

Kerry Lutz: It's clear the left's reaction has been intense. What are they planning?

Martin Armstrong: They're struggling to accept the outcome. I've heard of protests being planned for January, hoping to trigger a response that might label Trump as authoritarian if he calls in the National Guard. But that tactic won't work; people are just too exhausted by the political games.

Kerry Lutz: What about NATO and the neocons? Trump has made it clear he wants to pull out of wars, and they're not thrilled.

Martin Armstrong: Right. NATO has become a hub for retired neocons, and they're actively trying to raise money to keep the Ukraine conflict going. But Trump's election threatens that. They're also pushing to expand into Asia, which aligns with the globalist agenda from the WEF and other entities pushing for a unified global defense force. Trump's stance on reducing U.S. military involvement abroad is a direct challenge to them.

Kerry Lutz: Let's talk about the economy. With a massive national debt, can Trump really make a difference?

Martin Armstrong: Yes, but it requires out-of-the-box thinking. He's mentioned eliminating income tax, which could work if paired with tariffs. We need to consider innovative solutions, like debt-to-equity swaps, to restructure the national debt and reduce dependency on government borrowing. If we can eliminate unnecessary debt, interest rates could drop, benefiting everyone.

Kerry Lutz: And would that help with inflation and currency stability?

Martin Armstrong: Absolutely. Our current debt cycle inflates the economy more than printing money would. If we reduce debt and stabilize interest rates, we could ease inflation and improve economic health. Also, redirecting capital from debt obligations into productive investments would benefit the economy.

Kerry Lutz: So, can Trump make these changes with enough support?

Martin Armstrong: It depends. Trump understands debt restructuring from his own experience, which could be an asset. But there are entrenched interests, especially in banking, that prefer the debt cycle. It'll take strong leadership and support from the public to enact real change.

Kerry Lutz: It sounds like Trump's victory could be the beginning of significant change.

Martin Armstrong: Yes, and with his prior experience, he'll be ready to hit the ground running. This second chance could actually make him more effective than if he'd served consecutive terms. He's coming in with a clear plan, and that's crucial.

Kerry Lutz: Thanks, Martin, for sharing your insights! Looking forward to seeing you at the conference. For everyone listening, don't forget to check out ArmstrongEconomics.com and stay tuned for more updates. See you soon, Martin!

Martin Armstrong: Thanks, Kerry! Looking forward to seeing you tomorrow.

Key Takeaways:

1. **Election Aftermath:** Trump's decisive victory reflects public dissatisfaction with the economic challenges under the previous administration, despite efforts to discredit him.
2. **Policy Reversals:** Expect immediate changes in domestic and foreign policies, focusing on immigration reforms, economic adjustments, and reducing overseas military involvement.
3. **NATO and Neocon Resistance:** Trump's anti-war stance challenges neoconservative agendas and globalist ambitions, particularly in NATO and the WEF.
4. **Debt Restructuring and Tariffs:** Trump may propose eliminating income taxes and leveraging tariffs to reduce national debt and dependency on government borrowing.
5. **Global Sentiment Shift:** Growing global resistance to Western-dominated policies signals potential realignment in international relations and economic frameworks.

Final Thought:

Trump's return to office represents a pivotal moment in U.S. and global politics. His clear agenda for reform and focus on economic restructuring may challenge entrenched systems, but public and political support will determine the success of these transformative efforts.

THE CYCLES OF POWER AND ECONOMICS (FEBRUARY 3, 2025)

Interview Summary:

Martin Armstrong explores the economic and political landscape following Trump's first two weeks back in office with host Kerry Lutz. They delve into the consequences of tariffs, the inevitability of a recession, government corruption, the failures of institutions such as NATO and the DOJ, and the struggles of the financial system. They also discuss the debt crisis, stock market projections, cryptocurrency, and gold prices alongside broader concerns about judicial corruption and economic cycles.

Kerry Lutz: Welcome to *The Financial Survival Network*. I'm your host, Kerry Lutz. Joining us today is Martin Armstrong. We're going to discuss Trump's first two weeks, tariffs, the looming recession, and whether anything can be done to change the economic cycles. Marty, it's great to have you back on the show. Quite a couple of weeks, huh?

Martin Armstrong: Oh, yeah. The old Chinese curse—may you live in interesting times.

Kerry Lutz: Especially if you work for the FBI or the Department of Justice. Things are getting really interesting for them.

Martin Armstrong: They're finally facing consequences. People need to understand how government agencies work. NATO is a great example. It was created during the Cold War to counter communism, but communism fell. We don't really need NATO anymore. But I've seen internal memos where they discuss how to remain relevant. Their strategy? Fear. "Russia will invade Europe if Ukraine falls! Send us money!" It's all about keeping their jobs.

Kerry Lutz: So, it's all about self-preservation?

Martin Armstrong: Exactly. The same goes for every government agency. I saw it in the 80s after the 1987 crash. The SEC blamed the CFTC, and the CFTC blamed the SEC. I suggested merging them into one regulator. But Congress said, "We can't do that, we'd have to lay off 50,000 people."

Kerry Lutz: It's never about what's right for the people.

Martin Armstrong: No, it's about maintaining power. Government isn't Santa Claus; they don't care about protecting you. This is about them staying in control.

Kerry Lutz: And now the DOJ seems to be under scrutiny. Do you think it will fail?

Martin Armstrong: We'll see. As of last night, it looks like they eliminated USAID, which has been a deep-state slush fund for over 60 years. Kennedy started it during the Cold War, but now it's laundering money worldwide—financing lawfare against Trump, the Wuhan lab, even illegal immigration. This might be the first of many cuts. But can they really cut a trillion dollars off the budget?

Kerry Lutz: They could, but would they survive trying?

Martin Armstrong: Exactly. Look at what happened before 9/11. Rumsfeld testified that $2 trillion was missing from the Pentagon's budget. The next day, a plane hit the exact room where the records were kept. To this day, the Pentagon still can't account for trillions.

Kerry Lutz: And they keep failing audits.

Martin Armstrong: Yes, but if the IRS audits you and you say, "I lost my records," you'd be out of business. They apply different rules to themselves.

Kerry Lutz: Do you find any satisfaction in the purges happening at the FBI and DOJ?

Martin Armstrong: People don't realize how corrupt these agencies are. In my case, I attended a reverse proffer, where they try to convince you to take a deal. They knew the bank stole the money, but they wouldn't go after the bank. My clients sued the bank, and the government put a gag order on me to stop me from helping them. The bank returned the money, but no one was jailed, no fines—nothing.

Kerry Lutz: The banks always get protected.

Martin Armstrong: Exactly. I once asked a lawyer why no banker ever goes to jail. His response? "You don't sh*t where you eat."

Kerry Lutz: That's the reality in the Southern District of New York.

Martin Armstrong: One of the most corrupt jurisdictions in the country. Judges have been caught changing transcripts. If you or I tampered with court records, we'd go to prison. But in New York, the Second Circuit merely "suggested" judges stop doing it, saying they had no power to enforce the law.

Kerry Lutz: And Trump walked into that mess.

Martin Armstrong: Yes. His judge wasn't even a real judge—just an acting prosecutor. How did he end up handling the most significant case in New York?

Kerry Lutz: And yet, Trump won.

Martin Armstrong: That's what threw them. In D.C., they thought, "If we make him a felon, no one will vote for him." It backfired.

251

Kerry Lutz: So, what's the future for the judicial system? Can Trump clean it up?

Martin Armstrong: Not without major reforms. Right now, prosecutors can indict anyone without oversight. There needs to be a committee review before charges are filed. Otherwise, they will never admit mistakes—because it affects their careers. Public defenders are worthless. Look at General Flynn. He hired a law firm from D.C., and they refused to challenge the judge for fear of career repercussions.

Kerry Lutz: It's rigged.

Martin Armstrong: Completely. You have to hire an out-of-town firm to get a fair defense. New York law firms won't challenge judges. That's why when Trump was charged there, I knew he'd see the real New York—pure corruption.

Kerry Lutz: Moving on to investments—Trump seems interested in crypto. What's your take?

Martin Armstrong: Cryptocurrency isn't feasible long-term. Bitcoin was created by intelligence agencies. There's a 1996 white paper from the NSA describing it. If some "Japanese guy" invented blockchain, why isn't he suing for patent rights?

Kerry Lutz: And the stock market? You predicted 65,000 by 2032. Still on track?

Martin Armstrong: Yes. When the market was at 20,000, I projected 40,000. Now, 65,000 isn't just about market growth—it's about the dollar's declining purchasing power.

Kerry Lutz: Gold has hit record highs. Will it go over $3,000?

Martin Armstrong: Gold rises due to geopolitical instability. When the dollar strengthens, gold falls—unless there's war. Look at history:

gold jumped from $100 in 1976 to $400 in 1979, then soared to $875 when Russia invaded Afghanistan.

Kerry Lutz: And Europe?

Martin Armstrong: It's collapsing. Germany is shrinking. The EU is falling apart. As Europe crumbles, capital will flee to the U.S., pushing the dollar up further. The BRICS nations see this and are pulling away from U.S. control. The old financial order is dying.

Kerry Lutz: We covered a lot today. Thanks, Marty. Looking forward to your next insights.

Martin Armstrong: My pleasure. Stay safe.

Key Takeaways:

1. **Government Agencies Prioritize Self-Preservation:** Institutions like NATO and DOJ operate primarily to maintain relevance and funding, often using fear-driven narratives to justify their existence.
2. **Judicial and Legal System Corruption:** The legal system is deeply compromised, with prosecutors and judges prioritizing career security over justice. The Southern District of New York is particularly notorious for legal manipulation.
3. **Debt Crisis and Economic Instability:** The greatest economic threat is in the debt markets, not the stock market. Government borrowing continues to spiral out of control, creating an inevitable financial downturn.
4. **Stock Market and Gold Projections:** The stock market is projected to reach 65,000 by 2032, mainly due to currency devaluation. Gold will rise due to geopolitical instability and economic uncertainty.
5. **Bitcoin's Intelligence Agency Origins:** Bitcoin and blockchain technology were allegedly developed by

intelligence agencies as a long-term method of financial tracking and control.

6. **Europe's Economic Decline:** The European Union is on the brink of collapse, with Germany's economy shrinking and the Eurozone struggling. This will drive capital into the U.S., strengthening the dollar.

7. **Tariffs and Economic Policy Missteps:** Trump's economic approach, particularly regarding tariffs, is based on outdated models that don't fully account for global financial interdependencies.

8. **Judicial System Reforms Are Necessary:** Without structural changes, including independent review committees for indictments, judicial and prosecutorial misconduct will persist.

9. **U.S. Dollar Strengthening:** As European economies weaken and global uncertainty grows, the dollar will continue to strengthen, impacting international trade and markets.

10. **Future Recession and Market Shifts:** The global economic downturn is inevitable, driven by government mismanagement, rising debt, and geopolitical instability.

Final Thought:

The global economy is on the brink of major change. With governments clinging to power, judicial corruption rampant, and economic cycles in full motion, only those who understand history and the business cycle will be prepared for what's coming next.

CONCLUSION

Reflecting on the many discussions captured in this book, it is clear that Martin Armstrong is not just an extraordinary forecaster but an extraordinary human being. While many would understandably harbor resentment after being deprived of 11 years of their life by an unjust system, Martin holds no grudges. Instead, he has channeled his energy and intellect into helping people understand the economy, their finances, and what may lie ahead. His resilience and unwavering dedication to sharing knowledge are testaments to his character.

Martin's ability to identify and explain the cyclical nature of history and markets is unparalleled. From his Economic Confidence Model to his insights into global capital flows, his systems and theories have proven to be far more effective than virtually any other predictive tools available today. While no one can foresee the future with absolute certainty, Martin's track record of accuracy across decades of forecasts speaks volumes about the value of his work.

Through these discussions, we gain not only a deeper understanding of complex economic forces but also an appreciation for Martin's mission: to empower individuals with the tools and knowledge to navigate an increasingly uncertain world. It is now up to you, the reader, to determine how best to apply his teachings and insights. Whether you are an investor, a policymaker, or simply someone seeking to make sense of a complex world, Martin Armstrong's wisdom offers a unique and invaluable perspective.